KU-165-246

"*Gifts of Grace* is a beautifully written and biblically rich devotional that will help you to slow down, exhale your troubles, and really savor the miracle we celebrate each Christmas. Jared draws on the songs of the Advent season to frame ancient truths in delightfully fresh ways. Each chapter will lift your eyes above the end-of-year chaos to marvel at the immeasurable riches of God's grace. Read this book, and let your heart be filled with wonder at the gifts that Christ alone can give."

ADAM RAMSEY, Lead Pastor, Liberti Church, Gold Coast, Australia; Network Director, Acts 29 Asia Pacific; Author, *Truth on Fire*

"To think that our whole Christian lives—and all of eternity—will be spent discovering and enjoying the riches of God's grace is almost too good to be true. But it is true. And Jared shows us why in his beautiful new book. *Gifts of Grace* will open to you the wonders of the gospel and offer your heart what it desires most this Christmas."

KRISTEN WETHERELL, Author, *Humble Moms*; Co-author, *Hope When It Hurts*

"Each day throughout the Christian season, this book will remind you of a different gift that God himself has given us through the first Christmas. Each chapter is a gift presented in a fresh and compelling way to nourish our hearts and calm our fears."

TIM CHESTER, Crosslands Training; Author, *Enjoying God*

"As you read this day by day during the Advent season, you will encounter God's grace and see the gospel as our Lord's greatest gift to us. I look forward to reading through *Gifts of Grace* with my family as our Advent devotional, and know it will strengthen our love for the one who first loved us."

DEAN INSERRA, Lead Pastor, City Church, Tallahassee; Author, *Getting Over Yourself*

"What a Saviour we have! Each day we unwrap another staggering truth about the Jesus who calls us to follow him."

RICO TICE, Senior Minister (Evangelism), All Souls Langham Place, London; Author, *Honest Evangelism*

"A treat of a book. Here is a simple way to enjoy a beautiful gospel gift each day of Advent. You will find truth to treasure, hope to inspire, and fuel to prepare you for the coming of Jesus."

JONTY ALLCOCK, Pastor, Globe Church, London; Author, *Impossible Commands*

"Oftentimes the message of Christmas gets lost in our hurried culture, and we miss the reason for the season. *Gifts of Grace* is like a compass that recalibrates our souls toward Christ."

DR. DERWIN L. GRAY, Co-founder and Lead Pastor, Transformation Church; Author, *How to Heal Our Racial Divide*

"*Gifts of Grace* is the kind of grounding, perspective-shifting reflection my soul needs each year. It is joyful and grateful and worshipful because it is deep and focuses on who Christ is and what he has done, which is decidedly not seasonal but eternal. In this little book, Jared has reminded the unfestive and tired among us of the most profound reasons to celebrate the birth of Jesus."

BARNABAS PIPER, Pastor; Author, *Hoping for Happiness* and *Help My Unbelief*

"This Advent, allow Jared Wilson's words to speak to your soul and stir your imagination. With his typical eloquence and grace, Wilson weaves the lyrics of songs that have so captured our hearts every Christmas season with fresh gospel meditations. Get this book, gather with your family, and rekindle your love for Jesus."

DANIEL DARLING, Director, Land Center for Cultural Engagement; Columnist, *World*; Author, *The Characters of Christmas*

GIFTS

OF

25 Advent Devotions

GRACE

Jared C. Wilson

Gifts of Grace
© Jared C. Wilson, 2022

Published by:
The Good Book Company

thegoodbook.com | thegoodbook.co.uk
thegoodbook.com.au | thegoodbook.co.nz | thegoodbook.co.in

Unless otherwise indicated, Scripture quotations are from The Holy Bible, English Standard Version (ESV), copyright © 2001 by Crossway, a publishing ministry of Good News Publishers. Used by permission. All rights reserved.

All rights reserved. Except as may be permitted by the Copyright Act, no part of this publication may be reproduced in any form or by any means without prior permission from the publisher.

Jared C. Wilson has asserted his right under the Copyright, Designs and Patents Act 1988 to be identified as author of this work.

ISBN: 9781784985950 | Printed in the UK

Design by André Parker

Contents

Introduction

"For from his fullness we have all received,
grace upon grace."—John 1:16

Advent is about anticipation. As Christians approach the Christmas holiday, we use the preceding weeks to slow down and profoundly meditate on the staggering reality of the incarnation of the Son of God to deepen our sense of expectation and wonder—a sense undoubtedly felt by those who anticipated the Messiah's first coming. Participating in the Advent season is how we put ourselves, as it were, in their shoes. It is for this reason that churches observe traditional Advent liturgies, pastors preach Advent sermon series, families use Advent calendars or wreaths, and Christians read Advent devotional books like this one. All of this observance helps us focus more devotedly on—and please forgive the cliché—"the reason for the season."

But I will admit that when I was a child, though I was raised in a faithful Christ-following, church-going family (who even lit candles in an Advent wreath a few years in a row), my fleshly little heart was focused more on anticipating the gifts under the tree on Christmas Day than the miracle of the Word putting on flesh. And to be honest, I still struggle with a misdirected focus at Christmastime. I don't think I yearn inordinately for presents like when I was a child, but I still suffer from a childish impatience, an immature inability to be still, go slow, and embrace anticipation.

I think a lot of other people share this struggle too, if our drive-thru, self-serve, express-lane kind of culture is any indication. But impatience and "hurry sickness" and the inability to focus are not new phenomena.

I suppose this is how those nifty Advent calendars came about. Do you know the ones I mean? Sometimes they are made of flimsy paper or cardboard, but sometimes nicer ones are made of wood or some other sturdy material, and they usually feature 24 little doors, one for each day of Advent. And behind each little door is a little treat, a little gift. Sometimes the gift is a chocolate or other candy; sometimes it's a little toy or charm. The idea is that 24 little gifts spread out over the days of Advent can arrest one's attention and even build the sense of expectation for the bigger celebration on Christmas Day. I recently saw one jokester on Twitter say that Advent calendars help children "micro-dose" Christmas!

There's some truth to that, though. The daily gifts of a thoughtful Advent calendar can help us more fully absorb the resonance of this season—besieged as it is with all the festive bells and whistles that never seem to deliver on their promise of enchantment—and more fully enjoy the central gift of Christmas: Jesus the King, himself.

And this is the purpose of the collection of devotional readings you hold in your hand right now. I want us to think of them like an Advent calendar. Every day, we will open up a little door to rediscover one of the myriad gifts Christians receive through the coming of Christ and belief in his gospel. In John's Gospel, the apostle tells us that from the fullness of Christ flows "grace upon grace" (1:16). Jesus is indeed an unceasing fountain of grace for those united to him by faith. So day by day, we will consider one amazing grace after another.

To be clear, though, unlike the tiny treats or trinkets in an Advent calendar, none of these gifts of grace are even by themselves little! The treasure trove of Christ's gospel is a lot like a Narnian wardrobe. It looks small enough on the outside—perhaps even simple or manageable—but once you walk through it, you discover an entire parallel universe of wonder and glory.

The whole gospel of grace is like that, and each dimension of its glory is like that too. I have heard it said that the gospel is a pool shallow enough for a child to play in and at the same time deep enough to drown an elephant! But the bigness of each daily gift of grace that we examine will be building to something bigger still. And my prayer for you is that examining the diamond of the gospel facet by facet for the next 24 days will find you on Day 25 more awestruck and joy-filled about the glory of Christ our Lord. It is only by beholding Christ's glory, in fact, that we can be made like him (2 Corinthians 3:18).

> *"But grace was given to each one of us according to the measure of Christ's gift. Therefore it says, 'When he ascended on high he led a host of captives, and he gave gifts to men'." (Ephesians 4:7-8)*

1. A Thrill of Hope

Today's Gift: Hope

"Therefore, preparing your minds for action, and being sober-minded, set your hope fully on the grace that will be brought to you at the revelation of Jesus Christ."—1 Peter 1:13

"You can't sing Christmas carols yet!"

Thus began an email I once received while serving as a pastor of a small congregation in New England. The sender wasn't angry—just concerned. I puzzled over the directive, as it was the first time I could remember ever encountering such an assertion. The context gave the reasoning: because, I was told, Advent is about anticipating the birth of the Messiah, we shouldn't sing songs celebrating that birth until the Sunday after December 25th.

I confess this was a tall order for me, especially given that I live in a household that decorates for Christmas around the end of October and begins playing Christmas music nonstop before the end of November. "What do you mean, I can't sing Christmas carols yet?"

The concept of "advent," of course, refers to an arrival or a coming. At this time of the year, Christians redirect their focus to the spirit of anticipation of the first advent of Christ. We do this to affirm the incarnation more thoroughly and commemorate the beginning of the New Testament gospel story with more joy.

But I sometimes struggle with the way many Advent observances are conducted. The forbidding of songs about Jesus' birth before Christmas Day is one such practice. It just feels a bit too much like playacting to me. I know *why* these things are insisted upon—it allegedly better helps us get "in the spirit" of Advent and is thought to heighten the joys of Christmas Day observance. But I'm telling you, it's hard for me to act as if I'm waiting for the birth of the Messiah when I know he's already come and, indeed, has already been crucified, buried, and raised, and has ascended to where he came from!

I don't know about you, but I can't pretend every year that Jesus hasn't been born, even if doing so might help me muster up some extra-spiritual feelings. But there is one thing I can do that helps get me close to that pre-Christian sense of anticipation: I can think hard about the second coming of Christ—the one still ahead, the *second* advent.

In fact, the feelings most of us have right now about the state of the world and the sin, chaos, and brokenness that seem to reign everywhere we look is very much like the feelings of those who anticipated the first coming of the Messiah. "How long, O Lord?" is a cry that goes up throughout the Old Testament, a lament for the *shalom* of Eden, which was lost at the fall, and an expression of grief over the evil, suffering, and injustice continually pervading the earth. How in the world could the children of God before the time of Christ remain faithful year after year, decade after decade, century after century as the arrival of their righteous King seemed to be delayed?

And how in the world can we in the 21st century remain faithful as the Lord, in his second coming, appears to tarry? After seeing so much bloodshed on a daily basis and feeling so much heartbreak year after year, knowing that in so many places hostility to Christianity is always increasing, and knowing that for all the technological, medical, and other intellectual advances mankind can make, we are no closer to eradicating injustice in the world, much less death, how do we not give in to despair?

The answer is *hope*.

Before Christ's first coming, God's people hoped in God. And before Christ's second coming, God's people hope in God.

God had birthed this hope in the children of Israel through his past faithfulness and goodness to them, so much so that the psalmist could say, despite his depression, that he knew he would come to a place of praise again (Psalm 42:11); the prophet could say that the God he felt was giving him the silent treatment was nevertheless still his only hope (Isaiah 8:17); and the sufferer could say that *even if God killed him*, he would still hope in him (Job 13:15).

They didn't know how long it would take to get to their deliverance, but they knew in their bones that it was coming. And this is why the people of God in all times hope differently than the people of the world. When the world hopes, there is the prospect of unfulfillment. The world "hopes" something will happen, but they know it might not. That's not how God's people hope. Our hope comes with assurance (Hebrews 11:1), our hope abides (1 Corinthians 13:13), and our hope will "not put us to shame" or disappoint us (Romans 5:5). Why? Because our hope is not in other people or in the times or even in ourselves—these things always change and are all stained by the fall.

No, our hope is in God! In fact, our hope *is* God!

So I can sing Christmas songs on December 1 and still get close to feeling how those who wrapped themselves in messianic expectation felt before that first Christmas Day, because I know what it's like to feel the weight of the weariness of the world around me but be anchored by the sure and steady hope of the Messiah to come. In 1 Peter 1:13, the apostle Peter instructs us to set our hope *fully* on the grace that will be coming to us at the coming of Jesus. Our hope cannot be half-hearted like the world's because our King is tried and true. And Peter connects this hoping fully in grace to readiness for action and sobriety of mind. When people hope in things that may or may not be true, they can become lazy and muddled. But when we hope in Jesus, we find the reason and the energy to live and to think in ways that magnify Jesus.

And this is itself a gift from God. As Peter says earlier in the chapter, God "has caused us to be born again to a living hope" (1 Peter 1:3). And in giving us Christ by grace, God has also given us "the hope of glory" (Colossians 1:27).

Today, then, as you think about what may feel like a long road of Advent before you, remember that as tired or wounded as this season may find you, the day is coming—and not too far off now—when the blessed hope (Titus 2:13) will appear and you will be able to say, "I knew it all along!" If it helps you hope, you could even sing some Christmas carols today.

2. Faith Holds Wide the Door

Today's Gift: Faith

"For by grace you have been saved through faith. And this is not your own doing; it is the gift of God."—Ephesians 2:8

The central doctrine to true Christianity, distinguishing it from all other world religions and even false variations of itself, is justification by faith alone. The Protestant Reformer Martin Luther famously said that this doctrine is the article upon which the church stands or falls. And it is also the doctrine upon which the true celebration of Christmas rises or falls. Apart from faith, Christianity—and even Christmas—is merely aspirational.

This is what I mean: in all other religions and even irreligious systems of personal or cultural betterment, we find a system of weights and measures. The burden of improvement and transformation is on imperfect people, who cannot bear that weight. It is up to sinners, in this way of thinking, to make peace on earth.

Perhaps you see the problem already. The best of mere men, as the saying goes, are mere men at best.

In the Old Testament, we read about centuries of men and women who succeed and fail, rise and fall, triumph and, well, die. All of our Old Testament heroes are still sinners. As the author of Hebrews in the New Testament surveys the sum of their exploits, we notice that while ample approval is given for their hard work, what ultimately commends them all to God is not their efforts but their... faith (Hebrews 11).

Can it be that simple?

Actually, it's that hard. Because, if repenting of our self-righteous efforts and instead trusting in God were easy, more of us would do it! And those of us who do find ourselves saved by faith wouldn't still constantly struggle with repenting of our pride and self-trust.

Think about the Christmas story itself. If you were inventing a story out of whole cloth about the rescue of mankind from sin and death, wouldn't you be more inclined to write about human triumph and superior human wherewithal? Countless books and movies would testify yes. In fact, most of the cultural expectation of the Messiah's coming revolved around images of military might and violent revolution. The dominant picture would have been one of a valiant warrior on a powerful steed, sword in hand, with the blood of the Roman oppressors trailing behind him.

Instead, we get a baby in a manger. And when he grows up and makes his triumphal entry, it is not on a stallion with swords, but on a donkey with palm branches. And this King, while certainly triumphing over the forces of death and darkness, does so not initially by physical warfare but by physical sacrifice. The cross is where many would-be messiahs found their ambitions crushed. But the true Messiah's cross becomes a place of victory, proven further by his glorious resurrection three days later.

Our justification takes something slightly more out of reach than human ingenuity. It takes faith. And this is one reason why I know Christianity is true—we wouldn't have made this up! Salvation by faith makes too little of us and so much of God.

None of us are born with a natural inclination toward this self-denying reliance on God. But Hebrews 11:6 tells us that without faith, it is impossible to please God. Our good works can't do that. Our spiritual feelings can't do it. Our religious inspiration can't do it. To please God, we need the faith that we do not, in ourselves, have the capacity for. So where do we get it?

In case you thought the good news of Jesus could not get any better, have you ever considered that the very faith we need in order to be saved is itself given to us by God? This is what Paul says in Ephesians 2:8. The faith that justifies us is a gift from God!

We see this idea echoed in texts like Romans 12:3, where Paul says the measure of faith we have is "assigned" by God; and in 1 Corinthians 12:9, where we read that the Spirit is the one who gives us faith; and even in Acts 13:48, where we see that those who exercised saving faith were those who were "appointed" to do so by God. In Philippians 1:29, Paul says that it was "granted" to us to believe in Jesus. And in Hebrews 12:2 we are told that Jesus is the "founder" (in some translations, the "author") of our faith.

I know an idea like this can seem counterintuitive, if not offensive, to some. I'll be honest in saying that it used to seem objectionable to me too. I too much liked the idea that my choosing Jesus was born of my own good intentions, but this, ironically, was just another form of spiritual superiority that is antithetical to the truth of grace (God's *unmerited* favor).

But there's another way to look at the idea of saving faith itself being a gift that can actually expand our wonder at the good news. Think of it this way: giving us the faith we need to be saved is just one more incredible proof that God actually loves sinners! The good news is actually better than we think it is.

It is as if God is saying to us, *You need faith to please me. Here—have some faith.*

That's how gracious a giver our God is! Whatever he demands *from* us, he supplies *to* us.

This is an important gift to treasure this holiday season, because many of us will inevitably feel let down by an insufficient joy in the festivities. We get caught up in the busyness of preparations, and, before we know it, the presents are unwrapped and trash litters the floor, there are lots of dishes to wash, the same old Christmas songs and movies don't bring quite the rush of nostalgia we were hoping for, and we finish up tired and disappointed. And if we let ourselves down in not properly feeling Christmassy, surely we've let God down, right?

Instead, he says to us, gently but firmly, *I did not send my Son to be earned by your works or your feelings. I sent him to be received by faith.*

One of the lesser-known verses of the traditional carol "O Little Town of Bethlehem" tells us:

Faith holds wide the door,
The dark night wakes, the glory breaks,
And Christmas comes once more.

The power of Advent, of the miracle of Christmas itself, does not come to us through decorations and parties but through the door of faith. And it doesn't even have to be a big door—just an open one. Jesus himself says we don't need a big faith to move mountains; it can be a tiny faith (Matthew 17:20). Its object just needs to be true. As Luther said in his most famous hymn, what even defeats the devil is that "one little word."

You can find all the faith you need for all the days ahead—because God in his merciful love will give it to you.

3. For Sinners Here, the Silent Word Is Pleading

Today's Gift: Justification

"She will bear a son, and you shall call his name Jesus, for he will save his people from their sins."
—Matthew 1:21

This is a biggie for Day 3 of Advent, isn't it? Examining the treasure of justification today is like opening up that Advent calendar, expecting a chocolate truffle, and finding a diamond ring. But we won't save this truth, upon which the church stands or falls, for a later day because so much of what we will explore in the days ahead stems from this doctrine central to true Christianity. In fact, I think you'll have a happier Advent season by getting to the idea of justification as early and as often as you can!

One practice I try to adopt during this season (imperfectly, to be sure) is to look for reminders of the heavenly verdict of justification for sinners everywhere I can. Sometimes these are hard to come by in a world set on self-exaltation. Sometimes I have to strain to see them.

I'll give you one example from a lame Christmas movie that my family has made a part of our annual holiday ritual. *Fred Claus* is certainly no masterpiece of film, but there is one scene that gives me chills every time I see it. Fred is the older brother of Santa, and he's grown up, of course, in the shadow of his saintly sibling. Through circumstances too detailed to mention here, Fred finds himself reluctantly employed by his kid brother at the North Pole, initially in charge of sorting through all the files of all the kids in the world and determining whether they ought to be on the naughty or nice list.

Sympathizing with kids who struggle to be good and frustrated by his own inability to measure up to his brother, Fred ends up maniacally stamping every kid's file, "Nice." He is, in effect, legally declaring bad kids to be *good*.

I'll acknowledge it's a stretch to find a one-to-one correlation between this act of Christmas rebellion and the real doctrine of divine justification, but I can never help having my heart stirred a little. Why? Because I am a thoroughly naughty person whose file of sins would be too thick to review in one lifetime. But this record of debt against me has been wiped away in one fell swoop by the declaration of my divine Judge.

Not because of me.

But because of Christ.

When the angel visits Joseph to tell him that the unborn child carried by Mary is not the product of an illicit romance but rather the miraculous work of the Holy Spirit, one crucial detail of this revelation is in the stated purpose of this miracle. The angel even tells Joseph what the baby's name should be! The child will be called Jesus, a derivation of Joshua, which means "God saves." This is why the Son of God becomes incarnate—to save sinners.

This is the whole point of Christianity, and thus the whole point of Christmas.

Jesus did not come primarily to set a good example, though he certainly did that. And he did not come to give us solid ethics teaching, though he did that too. He didn't even come primarily to perform signs and wonders, though he undoubtedly did many. The primary reason for the incarnation was that God might justify sinners through Christ's sinless life, sacrificial death, and glorious resurrection.

To be justified is no small thing. It is why we are constantly defending ourselves, arguing our case (to others or even just in our own heads), rehearsing our good points, and just generally explaining ourselves all the livelong day. Even people who don't know Jesus inherently feel the need to justify themselves. And we all know, deep down, that this is a losing game. The more blame we shift and the more we prop ourselves up, the more empty and foolish we inevitably feel.

Now, to be justified before God is an even bigger thing. God is perfectly holy. He is the highest and greatest of all beings: the uncaused cause, the uncreated Creator, the unmoved mover, and the eternal source of all goodness and life. By contrast, we are not only small and weak, but, because of our sin, we fall guilty before him from birth. Because of our unholiness, we rightfully deserve condemnation from God.

But in a remarkable twist, we are told that God did not show up in human flesh simply to share that condemnation face to face. No, instead, John tells us this: "For God did not send his Son into the world to condemn the world"—again, the world already stood condemned!—"but in order that the world might be saved through him" (John 3:17).

Now, to be clear, we must be honest about the severity of our condemnation apart from God's grace, because the good news will only be as good as the bad news is bad. If God is only slightly disappointed in us, we can make do with a Jesus who came simply to tell us to get our act together. But if we are altogether unable to get our act together—if in fact we are deserving of death and hell with no innate resource to escape this fate— the idea of being justified by God in Christ is absolutely thrilling!

Justification is, of course, a legal term. It is a forensic declaration in which an accused person is categorized as "not guilty." In courts of criminal law, evidence of an accused person's guilt is presented by a prosecutor, arguments are made about appropriate sentences, and, of course, a defense is mounted in hopes of rebutting the prosecutorial case. The first hint of trouble for us, however, is that in the divine court of law, the evidence of our guilt is undeniable and overwhelming, and further, we have no real defense. Our excuses won't work. Our evidence of good behavior can never overcome the insurmountable debt we owe to the holy God, who demands our perfection and deserves our righteousness.

But unlike any other court in existence, in this court of divine law, the perfect Judge himself descends from the bench to stand in the place of the accused, offering his own virtue as a substitute for the righteousness needed for acquittal. Indeed, this Judge doesn't just offer his virtue; he offers his very life. He takes the sentence of death we deserve for the crimes we've committed against him. In this way, the Judge can maintain justice while simultaneously justifying the guilty (Romans 3:26).

And in this way, even a sinner like you can be free of your condemnation from God forever.

So I hope you'll forgive me having you open this gift so early. Some gifts are just so good that it doesn't make sense to wait to enjoy them.

4. Cast Out Our Sin and Enter In

Today's Gift: Expiation

"As far as the east is from the west,
so far does he remove our transgressions from us."
—*Psalm 103:12*

The difference between wanting to be completely rid of guilt and wanting to be completely rid of sin is no small thing. Every normal person desires to not feel guilty. But to desire not to be sinful? That's an entirely different matter.

This is part of what makes the good news so good. In the sacrifice of Christ on the cross, we not only have the atoning blood provided, which we need to be made right with God (justification), but part of that work is the opening of the door of our hearts to the indwelling power of the Holy Spirit, who comes to help us actualize the holiness bequeathed to us!

I think many of the ancient Israelites felt this difference keenly, if only because the sacrifices they offered for the atonement for sin had to be offered perpetually. Imagine that endless trail of blood flowing from the sacrificial altars, the stink of the carnage in the air, the gore of the whole process. While the sacrifices prescribed by God were received by him as pleasing to him, the whole messy process had to be a continual reminder to the ones making the sacrifices of the sheer offense of their unholiness.

In some rites, like that of the scapegoat, there was the picture not just of guilt being eradicated but the actual removal of sin, the casting out of unholiness, the vanquishing of their transgressions. In Leviticus 16:8-10, we see Aaron presenting one goat as a sin offering for atonement (indicative of the work of propitiation, to which we will turn our attention tomorrow) and another as a live offering for atonement, which was sent into the wilderness. The idea was that this scapegoat carried away the sins of the people, symbolically representing the casting away of their sin into the void.

What is illustrated in the exiling of the scapegoat and other rituals is the cry of a heart after God: "Pardon my guilt, yes, Lord, but please take this sin away from me!"

Psalm 103:12 gets at this desire. It is a promise to the redeemed that, because of the work of the Messiah and through the power of his Spirit, we can see our sin not just forgiven but also canceled and cast out. "As far as the east is from the west." The connotation here is a total vanquishing, a throwing of it into the void of nothingness. Elsewhere, we learn that God intends even to remember our sins "no more" (Hebrews 8:12, quoting Jeremiah 31:34). Another precursor to this idea is found in Micah 7:19, where the prophet says of God, "You will cast all our sins into the depths of the sea" (7:19b).

This is surely about God not holding our sin against us. But the language of "far as the east is from the west" and "no more" and "cast ... into the depths of the sea" speak not just to pardon but to removal.

The theological term for this is *expiation*. And that is the gift we ponder today. Expiation essentially means "a removal." But while the people of God before the coming of Christ had to re-enact this expiation constantly through the continual schedule of sacrifices, we know that those were just foreshadows of the perfect sacrifice to come. He has come! And he has done away once for all with the endless sacrifices (Hebrews 7:27; 9:26), as his cross announces that the work of expiation is finished (John 19:30).

Of course, we will not fully experience the total removal of sin until Christ's second Advent, when we finally see him face to face, finally knowing him the way he knows us (1 Corinthians 13:12). On that glorious day, we will see our sin climactically and eternally cast out of us. The cry of every redeemed heart will become true, as time itself will become one of a pure holiness reaching as far as east is from west.

Until then, in these days reflecting on the first Advent, we can be grateful for the work of God's Spirit, constantly bearing the fruit of holiness in our lives, gradually conforming us more and more to the image of Christ, and empowering us to repent of our sin and wage war against our flesh. The Messiah has come not just that we can be declared holy but so that we can actually be holy! And he is coming again, among other things, to satisfy the cry of the soul weary of sin.

It's not just our guilt that will be removed; it's our sin.

Aren't you tired of it? Don't you long to be free of the struggle?

Praise God that we have the gift of expiation, by which to battle sin with spiritual power, and praise God that every justified sinner will someday (and soon!) simply be *justified* and no longer a sinner.

5. By Thine All-Sufficient Merit

Today's Gift: Propitiation

*"In this is love, not that we have loved God
but that he loved us and sent his Son to be the
propitiation for our sins."*—1 John 4:10

Santa Claus is a big, fat legalist. He's a Pharisee in a festive hat. He is. Oh, he may seem jolly. He might enjoy cookies and milk, and playing with Rudolph, and frolicking around with the elves at the North Pole, but he's a full-on law-centered, judgmental moralist.

Here, I'll prove it to you: this guy supposedly spends his entire year, not just preparing to deliver toys for Christmas Day, but spying on every kid in the world, making sure they measure up to some arbitrary standard of reward. He makes a list! And he checks it twice. That's how hyper-focused he is on dividing kids into categories of "good" and "bad." If you're good, you'll get that shiny new bike or pretty new doll. If you're bad, you'll get a lump of coal or a sack of rocks.

And how do you know if you've been good enough to get off that bad list? You don't. You can never know. You just have to try your hardest and hope for the best.

Like I said—legalist.

While we played Santa with our two daughters when they were growing up, my wife and I wanted it to feel more like a kind of make-believe. We never told them Santa Claus was watching them, and we certainly never told them that if they weren't good, he wouldn't bring them anything. And we figured that when they grew old enough, they'd naturally tire of the make-believe, and that acknowledging Santa is a fairy tale wouldn't crush their little hearts. We were right.

But one reason why we didn't do the whole "Santa's making a list" thing had less to do with fear of deceiving our kids about a jolly old elf whom we only talked about at Christmastime and more to do with realizing that they—and you and I and everyone else we know—live in a world of insurmountable law. We swim constantly in a sea of merit and judgment. The entire world relates to most of us based on our performance, our looks, our abilities, and our contributions. And I don't think we need to exacerbate the felt pressure of that experience if we can help it, and certainly not at a time of year when we are trying to focus on the invasion of goodness and grace into this bad and broken world.

Have you figured out yet that there's just no satisfying the demands of a world that is set to accept you only so far as you measure up to its ever-changing standards?

And here's the really strange thing: satisfying the legalistic powers of the world, religious or secular, is always out of reach despite the fact that the powers of the world themselves do not measure up to any standard of perfection. The only perfection that exists is God himself. And the one and only holy God—get this—makes satisfaction reachable. Not *by us*, mind you. But by him, for us.

The gift we open today is *propitiation*. The concept of propitiation is very similar, actually, to that of expiation, which we looked at yesterday. Both are aspects of justification, and both have to do with the way God deals with our sin. In that respect, expiation and propitiation are very closely related and somewhat inextricable from each other. But while expiation entails forgiveness by the removal or cleansing of sin, propitiation entails forgiveness by satisfying the judgment of the wronged party.

What we see in a composite portrait formed from both the Old Testament rituals and the New Testament's fulfillment of them in the work of Christ is that Jesus became the propitiating sacrifice for sinners. In other words, at the cross, Jesus took the punishment sinners deserve in order to satisfy the wrath of God justly due to them.

Now, we have to be careful here, because sometimes people promote the important doctrine of propitiation in unhelpful and unbiblical ways. For instance, sometimes the image is presented of a wrathful Father whose arm is twisted, as it were, by the gracious Son. Such an idea depicts an unbiblical division within the Trinity and even reflects the spirit of some ancient heresies related to the will of God. So it will not do to imagine an angry Father who must be persuaded by a loving Son not to hate the Son's brothers and sisters.

Rather, because the Father and the Son (and the Spirit) share the same essence, they share the same divine will. (Hang with me here; I promise I won't get too academic.) Thus, we can rightly say that the entire triune Godhead is holy enough to hate sin and mete wrath to sinners and, at the same time, is loving enough to want to forgive sin and reconcile sinners to the Godhead. To act with perfect justice, God must punish sin. (God cannot break his own rules, not even for rule-breakers, because he is holy.) But, in an act of perfect love, God was able to both satisfy justice and forgive sinners. How? By performing the satisfaction for them: sending the Son as a substitute to pay the debt they owe and die in their place.

Sometimes propitiation is defined as "a payment that makes the receiver favorable." As I alluded to previously, this definition is a little imprecise as it relates to the gospel, because it was out of a favorability toward his sinful elect (his chosen people) that God sent his Son to make the payment in the first place. But it's still an accurate statement to say that the willing sacrifice of Jesus satisfies God's wrath and, at the same time, demonstrates God's love toward sinners (Romans 5:6-8).

This is the point John is making in 1 John 4:10, when he says, "In this is love, not that we have loved God but that he loved us and sent his Son to be the propitiation for our sins." The Christ child was not sent out of anger but out of love. The baby Jesus was not born to condemn the world but to bring salvation to it (John 3:17). And the Father is not some miserable miser needing to have grace for us pried from his stingy fists. He had determined from eternity past that even though he knew his creatures would rebel against his holiness, he would give of himself out of a great love to save them.

And if he was disposed to do this from eternity past, and if this love was confirmed and expressed climactically in the satisfaction realized by the cross of Christ, do you know what this means for you today? It means God's not mad at you.

No more hoops; no more hurdles. You don't have to measure up or earn his favor. He's not holding out on you. He is eternally pleased with you—not because of your sacrifices but because of Christ. The cross really was a propitiation. But if God's waiting on you to impress him, withholding love from you based on your performance, or "losing his temper" (so to speak) at your every screw-up, then the cross really wasn't a propitiation.

But it was. God himself says so.

Because of the Messiah and his atoning work, then, God is satisfied and delighted with you. That's what propitiation is all about.

And if Santa doesn't like it, he can put it in his chimney and smoke it!

6. Goodwill Henceforth from Heav'n to Men

Today's Gift: Peace

"Glory to God in the highest, and on earth peace among those with whom he is pleased."
—Luke 2:14

As we near the end of the first week of December, how are you feeling? Are you thinking about all the things you need to get done before a holiday break? Projects to finish, reports to finalize, gifts to buy, social engagements to attend, cards to send, travel plans to make? Feeling a little overwhelmed?

It's a strange irony that for many of us, what we look forward to as a great festive respite from the hustle and bustle of normal life turns out to be even more hustle-ly and bustle-ly than any other time of the year! I was speaking with a friend recently about our shared love for the Christmas season, but I confessed to him that I often turn the corner toward the new year feeling worn down and chewed up. Every year I feel as though I'm dragging myself across the finish line into January 1. And this fatigue—and even anxiety—begins to wear on me in the first week of

December, as I contemplate all the obligations and appointments that lie ahead.

I don't know if you feel like that right now, but it's likely that you have felt like that more than once throughout the past year. Social scientists and psychologists have been warning us that the rates of anxiety and depression are increasing at staggering rates every year. Maybe you read Bible verses like Luke 2:14 and think, "Peace on earth? Okay, I'll take it. But how?"

One idea I've had to—forgive the expression—*make peace* with is that the reality of God's peace doesn't necessarily (or even usually) eradicate the world's agitation. Sometimes God stills the raging storms outside, but more often than not, he has his eyes more set on the storms inside. "Peace I leave with you," Jesus says to his disciples in John 14:27; "my peace I give to you. Not as the world gives do I give to you. Let not your hearts be troubled, neither let them be afraid." And then later, in John 16:33 "I have said these things to you, that in me you may have peace. In the world you will have tribulation. But take heart; I have overcome the world."

Notice that Jesus is not promising that everything in his disciples' lives is going to be smooth sailing now that they are following him. He doesn't promise peaceful circumstances. Instead, he speaks peace to their hearts.

Jesus does not promise that earth will be heaven before his second coming, but he does promise that the kingdom of heaven can fill our hearts before then. And if we're going to have to keep living for a while in this world of trouble, what could be better than to know we are citizens of heaven in the meantime?

Notice the way the angelic announcement of peace in Luke 2:14 is actually phrased. We are used to hearing it as "Peace on earth, goodwill to men." Instead, the text actually says, "Peace among those with whom he is well pleased." In other words, the first advent does not bring peace upon the earth in the sense of eradicating wars, overturning injustice, solving poverty, squelching envy and rivalry, and the like. What the first advent brings to those stuck in the tragic brokenness of all those things is the spiritual peace of justification before God. The angel says the peace is coming to people with whom God is pleased. It does not—and cannot—come to those who do not repent of their sin and put their faith in Jesus the Messiah.

Why?

Because only those who know Christ can truly know peace. He ushers us into his kingdom of blessing for peacemakers (Matthew 5:9). His sacrifice ends the hostility between God and sinners (Ephesians 2:14-16). His resurrection conquers the threats of death and hell.

Look, you may not be able to avoid the stress of the holiday season without canceling everything, running away, and becoming a hermit. (Honestly, this option seems more and more appealing to me each year!) So you're probably up for another year of busyness and burdens. But one of the gifts we receive from the fullness of Christ is the spiritual fruit of peace (Galatians 5:22). You don't have to be on edge or riddled with worry this Christmas. It's actually one of the beauties of daily Advent meditations like these that the child of God can slow down and take a deep breath, but, more importantly, can also reflect on the truth that the most important things that threaten us have been eternally settled because of Christ.

Even the prophecy of Christ's birth speaks to the depths of this reality. "For to us a child is born, to us a son is given," Isaiah 9:6 says; "and the government shall be upon his shoulder, and his name shall be called Wonderful Counselor, Mighty God, Everlasting Father, Prince of Peace." Each of these titles ascribed to the coming Messiah builds into the final designation of Prince of Peace. Because of the counsel we receive from the Spirit and our eternal adoption of us by our heavenly Father—because of the sovereign omnipotence of God!—Christ, the Son of God, can be to anxious, frazzled, busy-sick sinners like us the Prince of Peace.

Today, put your cares on his shoulders. He can carry them. Give thanks to God for his peace, which is greater than your understanding, and ask him to guard your heart and mind with it (Philippians 4:7).

7. God and Sinners Reconciled

Today's Gift: Reconciliation

"All this is from God, who through Christ reconciled us to himself and gave us the ministry of reconciliation."—2 Corinthians 5:18

Family conflict is a ruiner of holidays. There are lots of jokes made about difficult relatives, but the reality of family trouble isn't really funny at all. When there is a rift between family members, it gives what ought to be a joyous and comfortable occasion a bitter taste, a dark shadow. When we know two feuding family members will both be present for the dinner party, we get a pit in our stomach. We remember what it was like the last time. The cold silence or the loud arguing. Everybody walking on eggshells. If you've done it before, you never want to try it again.

Maybe you're already dreading the upcoming holiday. Maybe you've even thought about staying home rather than spending time and money traveling to a family get-together that you know will be less than peaceful.

Sometimes, when I think of family conflict, I think of the biblical origins of it. Adam and Eve freshly divided from each other by their sin. Cain and Abel. Jacob and Esau. Joseph and his brothers. And much later, the so-called "prodigal son" and his older brother in Jesus' parable.

I think most of us can relate in a few ways to that latter story. We all have that "wild child" relative whose life seems to go crossways from the rest of the family. We all have that parent or grandparent or aunt or uncle who, like the father in the story, patiently waits and earnestly forgives. And we've probably all been, from time to time, that older brother following the rules, minding the store, doing our best while resenting our less conscientious relatives getting the umpteenth chance to start over. If we live long enough, I think most of us get a chance to be all three characters in the story.

Jesus' parable presents the ancient recipe for family conflict. And while there is a sweet scene of reconciliation between the patient father and his once-lost son, there is no tidy resolution to the tale. We don't know if the older brother has a change of heart—if he in fact repents of his envy and bitterness and comes to share his father's heart for his repentant sibling. And so it kind of leaves the question of full reconciliation open ended.

I think this unresolved conclusion makes a larger point about the reconciliation sinners experience through the gospel. For instance, have you ever noticed that the parable of the lost son is preceded by two other parables—the lost sheep and the lost coin—both of which include someone actively looking for that which is lost? The shepherd goes to look for the lost sheep. The woman sweeps the house looking for the lost coin. But nobody goes to look for the lost son. Why?

I wonder if the unstated conclusion that we are supposed to draw is that Jesus is the true fulfillment of the faithful older brother? Throughout the Scriptures, we keep getting these portraits of cruddy older brothers: ones who tarnish their family legacies, fail to live up to the expectations that come with receiving their birthright, and treat their younger siblings like dirt. This trend culminates in the parable's older brother, opening the door to our faithful big brother, Jesus.

When you think about it, what the older brother doesn't do in Jesus' story makes total sense. The younger brother is the one who has messed up. He's the one who treated his father like he wished he was dead. He's the one who wastes his time, his money, and his life. He's the one who ought to take responsibility for everything. As he left his older brother in the lurch, leaving him to do the work of two sons and comfort their father besides, he's the one who should be pursuing reconciliation. But what's amazingly gracious about the true story of the gospel is that the offended party (Jesus) doesn't wait for the offenders (us) to wise up, clean up, and shape up. Instead, the one we've sinned against takes the initiative to seek us out while we're still wallowing in our sin.

Paul writes in 2 Corinthians 5:18 that God through Christ reconciled us to himself. The Father sent the Son to rescue the wayward children. The older brother in the parable treasured his own sense of "being right" more than he did things in his family being *made* right. Jesus set aside the comforts of his heavenly home to reach us out in the wilderness. He is the good older brother who goes to find the younger brother and do the work of reconciliation—work we ought to do but can't: work he shouldn't have to do but does.

And Jesus doesn't face tension in the kitchen, arguments in the living room, and awkwardness around the dinner table. Jesus stared down a crown of thorns, a cat-o'-nine-tails, the centurion's spear, and the cross of Golgotha. He endured it all. Just to bring us home. "And you, who once were alienated and hostile in mind, doing evil deeds," Paul writes, "he has now reconciled in his body of flesh by his death, in order to present you holy and blameless and above reproach before him" (Colossians 1:21-22).

This Advent, whatever you're preparing to face in your own family, think of what Christ has done to make you a part of his. There's power in the reconciliation of the gospel. There's a gift there too—a gift to be shared in the "ministry of reconciliation" (2 Corinthians 5:18).

8. O Come, All Ye Faithful

Today's Gift: The church

"Here there is not Greek and Jew, circumcised and uncircumcised, barbarian, Scythian, slave, free; but Christ is all, and in all."
—Colossians 3:11

Do you believe that your church is a gift? Not just *the* church. *Your* church. The local assembly of believers that you attend in person. The one with the messy people, the awkward people, the weird people. The one with the pastor you wish was a little more gifted at some things and a little less prone to others. *That* church. It's a gift.

Yes, of course, there are bad churches out there—places that have become corrupt with unrepentance or tainted by heresy, or have even been infiltrated by abuse. But the normal, garden-variety congregation, warts and all, is a gift of God to the Christian.

So I'll ask you again: Do you believe your church is a gift?

It's difficult to think that way when we've set our minds on the deficiencies of those around us. We might think the preaching should be better or the music more engaging. We might think the people could be more welcoming, more hip, or just more numerous. But when we rehearse in our own minds the faults and failings of the people with whom we share church membership, we practically forget the good news that put us all together in the first place. We might not have picked this family for ourselves, but God did. And his ways are infinitely wiser than ours.

The church is a very peculiar community, isn't it? As with our blood family, we don't really get to choose who's in and who's out. But unlike all of our blood family, we'll have to live with our brothers and sisters in the faith for all eternity!

We should probably start figuring out how to do that now.

Colossians 3:11 gives us a portrait of a family based entirely on the blood of Christ. There ought to be no advantage in the church to being of a particular ethnicity or from a particular earthly family, or holding any other social or cultural currency. This is not the way many of our churches conduct themselves, sadly, but in reality, every member of a church is equally a child of God and equally, with every other member, a co-heir of the grace of Christ. And this makes the church unlike any other organization or community. Christ has come to call people of every tribe, tongue, race, and nation to share in the goodness of himself and the blessings of his kingdom. And the only thing qualifying sinners for this heavenly citizenship is saving faith.

The gift of faith makes the gift of the church vitally real and utterly unique.

Of any other organization and community, people can say, "Well, sure. It makes all the sense *in the world* that those people would be together." And of course that makes sense *in the world*. But the church is a heavenly reality. It is a gift from God. People from all kinds of families, social backgrounds, cultural contexts, political affiliations, and personal experiences—all bought by the blood of Christ, mystically united to him, serving out his mission on earth and, at the same time, seated with him in the heavenly places (Ephesians 2:6).

And so your church should be a place only explainable by the gospel. People should look at our churches and think, "There must be something to this God thing, to this gospel thing. There's no other explanation of why *those* people would get together, much less actually love each other."

Our churches should be a living apologetic for the strange reality of grace.

And in fact, our collective experience of unity—our collective *display* of unity—is vitally connected to our individual and collective union with Christ. This is what Jesus refers to in his high-priestly prayer, when he says to the Father, "I in them and you in me, that they may become perfectly one, so that the world may know that you sent me and loved them even as you loved me" (John 17:23).

That last part just slays me. Jesus is saying to the Father that he wants sinners like us to know that the

Father loves us *just as he loves Jesus.* Undeserving people like us are loved by the Father just as the holy Son is loved by the Father. I just can't get over that.

And the church is the place where we get to revel in that amazing truth, rehearse that truth, and remind each other of that truth. That's hard to do when we're expecting everybody to measure up to our preferences and expectations. It's hard for us to do when we're expected to measure up to everybody else's, isn't it?

Today, as you reflect on the gift that, yes, even your church is to you, contemplate this question: how will the world in need of Christ know the gospel is true? By the Holy Spirit, of course (and more on that tomorrow). But also, as Jesus indicates in his prayer, through the oneness of the church. The unity of the church is a testimony to the truth of the gospel.

The church is, in fact, a family made by the gospel. The grace of God has come in and through Jesus to call all kinds of people to be reconciled to God—and to each other—so that we together magnify his glory. In the gospel, strangers aren't just made into friends. Enemies are made into brothers and sisters. What a wonder! And what a gift to celebrate on this eighth day of Advent.

9. That Hath Made Heaven and Earth of Naught

Today's Gift: Power

"His divine power has granted to us all things that pertain to life and godliness, through the knowledge of him who called us to his own glory and excellence."—2 Peter 1:3

Throughout Advent, we are preparing our hearts to celebrate the reality of the incarnation, which was the opening salvo in heaven's invasion of earth. It seems at first like a rather inauspicious way to begin a revolution, doesn't it? If you're trying to overthrow one powerful kingdom with another, would you really think of sending... a baby?

It would not have been entirely out of the question for the Son of God to have manifested as a fully grown man. After all, we assume that Adam was created as a physically mature adult. But in order to, first, endure the entirety of the human experience and, second, subvert the cultural expectations of a messianic coronation, Jesus was conceived by the Holy Spirit in the womb of a virgin and breathed his first breaths of air in a musty animal pen. Is this how a king enters the scene?

Yes. And, in fact, it's how heaven enters the earth.

Just think about it: a newborn baby boy, helpless and barely conscious of himself or of others. Is there any more vulnerable person in the world? Next to an *unborn* child, the most vulnerable person in our world is probably a newborn child. A newborn is completely reliant on others for food, warmth, and shelter. A newborn cannot protect him- or herself, and without care, will die.

So here we are, preparing to celebrate the moment the God of the universe—omnipotent, omniscient and omnipresent—came into the world as *that*.

It really is a wonder, isn't it? The same fresh soul that had yet to grow in wisdom and stature (Luke 2:52) also held the mind that conceived of all we know and see, and more. The babyfat fists that wagged in uncoordinated baby spasms belonged to the one who also upheld the universe by the word of his power (Hebrews 1:3).

We know all of this because Jesus was fully God from birth. He did not become God later. He was not born partly God and then ascended to fullness of deity later. No, the fullness of deity dwelled in him bodily (Colossians 1:19; 2:9), even as a newborn.

The little baby figure in your little nativity scene is a symbol of the greatest power in existence—the divine might of omnipotence—humbling himself to come and reside with us. And the very fact that we are remembering and celebrating "God with us" is a reminder that his power is working in and through and with us too.

No, we cannot wield divine power as God does. No, we cannot manipulate or leverage that power. But the very truth of God's dwelling presence—Immanuel, "God with us"—is also the truth of God's *in*dwelling presence. For sluggish, tired, burdened believers, to know that the Holy Spirit has taken up residence not just in a stinky barn but in stinky people is an enduring and unconquerable encouragement.

The apostle Peter writes:

> *"His divine power has granted to us all things that pertain to life and godliness, through the knowledge of him who called us to his own glory and excellence, by which he has granted to us his precious and very great promises, so that through them you may become partakers of the divine nature." (2 Peter 1:3-4)*

This is same power that created the world *ex nihilo* ("out of nothing"). The same power that conceived a child in the womb of a virgin. The same power to raise the dead from the grave. The same power to transform a sinful heart—to make dead-in-sin people born again. This is the same power that indwells the life of Christians.

This stunning spiritual reality is what prompts Peter to declare that we are "partakers of the divine nature." Again, we can't wield God's power, as if we were gods ourselves. Peter does not say that we are partakers of the divine *essence*. But we do have power from on high that connects us to the goodness and glory of God in a life-changing way. We have power now to get up each morning with joy. We have power now to endure even the greatest suffering with a greater hope. We have power now to repent of sin and withstand the temptation of the devil. We have power now to experience the greatest reality humans could ever experience—to know and be known by God as our Father. To be friends with Jesus.

His divine power has granted to us all things ultimately worth having. What an amazing gift of grace, that people like us could know the power of God!

10. Wonders of
His Love

Today's Gift: Love

"And Jesus, looking at him, loved him"
—Mark 10:21a

Sometimes I think I can earn God's acceptance of me. I mean, I'm not one of those prosperity-gospel types—I don't believe that my faith will make me healthy or rich. Except, in a way, this is sometimes exactly what I believe. Because the prosperity gospel is just an extreme form of self-righteousness, I'm embracing a weird form of this false teaching whenever I imagine that God's love for me increases or decreases based on how I'm performing as a Christian. Whenever I turn my faith in Jesus into a formula and God's favor into a component of a mathematical equation, earned by my works, I've become a kind of prosperity gospelist. As with the prosperity gospel, I am believing that God's best rewards are contingent on me.

I know that I believe this, because my first instinct when something goes wrong in my life is to wonder what I've done to upset God. I wonder if I haven't given enough to the church, been engaged in enough daily prayer, or read my Bible with quite enough intensity. Maybe, I think, the Lord is punishing me because I haven't been quite as religious as I ought to have been.

Jesus constantly encountered people who thought like this. And when I notice that in my Bible reading, I pay very close attention. I want to know how he treated them. In Mark 10, for instance, the guy we know now as a rich young ruler comes up to Jesus and asks him, "What must I do to inherit eternal life?" (Mark 10:17).

Already we can see the young man is a bit off track. He wants to know what he has to *do* to inherit eternal life. He surely knows that sons of wealthy men don't work for their inheritances; they receive them simply by virtue of being sons! But Jesus engages with him along these lines of works-righteousness anyway, and eventually he cuts to the heart of the young man's idolatry. The young enquirer wants Jesus to receive everything he is *willing* to give. But Jesus knows the one thing he holds most dearly in his heart; he knows what the young man's idol is—his money.

As far as we know, the rich young ruler goes away not just distressed but also disbelieving. The whole scenario serves as a warning. But it also serves as a great stirring—at least, it does to me. This man is presenting his works-righteousness to Jesus. He is parading his self-righteousness, pleading his case. *Surely, I've earned the right to God's favor!* he's saying.

And while Jesus is prepared to burst the bubble of his self-inflated religiosity, he doesn't do so out of malice or disdain. No—in fact, Mark 10:21 tells us that "Jesus, looking at him, loved him." Even in this man's unbelief, even in his self-righteousness, even in his pride, even in his stupidity—Jesus loved him.

The "looking at him" part is notable, as well. Jesus wasn't weighing the man's works to see if he had earned enough credit to be loved. He was certainly about to call the man to repentance, because he knew what idol was keeping the man from truly *loving Jesus*. But there was nothing the rich young ruler could do to merit Jesus' love. The Savior saw him as he was. He saw the sin beneath the surface. He saw him in his idolatrous state. He saw the real man, not the polished version of himself which the man wanted Jesus to accept.

And the same is true for us. Jesus doesn't love some put-together, religious version of us. In our lowest, meanest, most desperate moments, Jesus sees us. At all times, he sees through our facades, through the makeup we put on so we look spiritual to everybody else, and through the personal avatars we send to church each Sunday hoping, everyone else will be fooled and impressed. He sees through it all, and he sees the real us. And he loves us.

I don't know where December 10 finds you. Maybe you're feeling overwhelmed by all you have to do to prepare for the holidays. Maybe you're feeling anxious about spending time with difficult family members. Maybe you're just feeling disappointed in yourself for not feeling sufficiently sentimental or spiritual or "Christmassy." Remember that no matter what kind of religious mathematics you bring to your experience of the holiday, Jesus loves you.

He loves you no matter what. He's not waiting for you to show your Christmas spirit. He's not waiting on you to jump through the holiday hoops to prove your worthiness. And he's certainly not expecting you to earn his grace. It is a free gift. He actually, truly, genuinely loves you.

And this is why he came: to show us this love face to face. To look us in the face that we might see *his* face and see in it nothing but love. And while we may not see him now after his ascension, he is still incarnate (though risen and glorified), and we will see him soon—indeed "face to face" (1 Corinthians 13:12). And we will know we are loved forever, no matter what.

11. God Imparts to Human Hearts the Blessings of His Heaven

Today's Gift: Imputation

"For our sake he made him to be sin who knew no sin, so that in him we might become the righteousness of God."—2 Corinthians 5:21

A few years ago I traveled by plane with my wife and two daughters to Houston to be with family during the Christmas holidays. It was on that trip that I discovered something surprising about the benefit known as TSA pre-check. Have you heard of this? It's a feature that allows someone to skip the long security lines at US domestic airports, opt for metal detectors instead of those sketchy full-body scans, and not have to remove shoes, laptops, or jackets when doing so. The security line is always much shorter, and the process is always much quicker. I love it.

Now, to acquire the TSA pre-check benefit, I had to find a local office, make an appointment, submit to an interview and a deep background check, and, of course, pay a fee. When everything cleared, I was given what's called a Known Traveler Number (KTN), and I use this number when booking flights to secure my pre-check status. But on this Christmas journey, I learned something new about the program—when I booked our family's itinerary using my name and applied my KTN to my ticket, the benefit extended to my wife and daughters too.

I have to tell you, this made getting through the airport so much easier. The ladies in my family carry so much stuff! And we weren't slowed down by having to sort through any of it over those little conveyor belts under the watchful eyes of some 20-year-old kid in a blue uniform and a delusion of grandeur. (Also, I didn't have to feel guilty about watching my girls go through lengthy security lines while I breezed through the pre-check line right next to them. I don't give up my TSA status for anybody!)

After all I'd gone through to secure this benefit, I was pleasantly surprised to find that it was automatically extended to my family, though they'd done nothing to earn it. I had done all the work. But when they traveled with me, my status got applied to them, and they were treated just as I was treated.

I hope you'll forgive the clunky metaphor here, but today's gift of the gospel is a little like that. The theologians call it the imputation of Christ's righteousness. It is the concept alluded to in 2 Corinthians 5:21 and other Scriptures where the perfect obedience of Jesus is said to be credited to us. Through our faith alone, we are not simply forgiven for our sins (as wonderful and as true as that is!); we are also counted as righteous (Romans 4:5; Galatians 3:6). You may have heard at some point that to be justified means, in effect, that it's "just as if I'd" never sinned. But in the light of imputation, to be justified also means "just as if I'd" always obeyed!

What did we do to earn being clothed in the righteousness of God? Nothing. Jesus has done all the work of qualifying us. And then, by virtue of simply being connected to him, we receive the benefit of the status he alone has proven worthy of.

The only thing we bring to this exchange is our need—indeed, our sin. In fact, 2 Corinthians 5:21 alludes to this dynamic, often referred to as the Great Exchange. At the cross, all of our sin and the condemnation it deserves was imputed to Jesus. He received it as if it was his own, despite the fact that he had done nothing to deserve that. "He made him to be sin who knew no sin," Paul says. And in exchange, Christ's righteousness is imputed to us—credited to our account, declared to be our own—despite the fact that we have done nothing to deserve that. In effect, we "become the righteousness of God."

And this means that the rights due to the Son extend to us. We are considered "co-heirs" with Jesus of the coming kingdom. His own resurrection has become the firstfruit of our resurrection to come. Even his joy is given to us. His peace is given to us. And he promises that the inheritance of eternal life in heaven will be given to us. "Where I am you may be also" (John 14:3).

All of the blessed benefits of being a Christian can be connected to the truth of the imputation of Christ's righteousness. As wonderful a gift as the forgiveness of sins is, can you also see how the splendor of the gospel is enhanced and amplified by the further gift of being counted righteous in him?

The imputation of Christ's righteousness is a beautiful reminder of just how exceedingly gracious our God is. He supplies to us what he demands from us. So along with the command to be holy as he is holy (Leviticus 11:45) comes the promise that he will give us his own holiness as a covering (Psalm 132:9)—"just as if" we'd always obeyed.

We are now clothed in his righteousness forever. Because of this, in a way, when God looks at us now, he sees his own Son. The gift of imputation is the gift of approval and acceptance. We are not treated according to our sin but according to the sinlessness of Jesus.

12. Sages, Leave Your Contemplations

Today's Gift: Wisdom

"[In Christ] are hidden all the treasures of wisdom and knowledge."—Colossians 2:3

Do you ever feel like you're the smartest person in the room? If so, I'd love for you to tell me what it's like because I literally never feel that way. Ever. If I was babysitting toddlers, I would be utterly convinced they would be minutes from pulling a fast one on me and escaping.

And I frequently feel this way where I work. I spent over 20 years in various church ministry roles, all without a seminary degree, before I was invited to come serve at a seminary. I was instantly intimidated. Why were the smart people asking me to come work for them?

Several years later, I've mostly gotten the hang of seminary work—and even got that degree in the process—but I don't feel all that much smarter. I am privy to conversations I cannot meaningfully join because I do not know the lingo. I witness debates I cannot substantively enter because I don't understand the terms. Even when I am teaching, I am conscious of the fact that I am regularly lecturing students who are more educated or otherwise much smarter than me.

I ought to be a nervous wreck every day of my life. But instead, I submit my anxiety about my intellect to the wisdom of my Savior. And I rejoice in the fact that while he may not have made me the smartest guy, he has still, through my faith in Jesus, opened up to me the greatest wisdom that exists in the universe. And if you are a Christian, he's done that for you too.

See, here's the difference. There are a lot of smart Christians out there, to be sure. Some of the smartest people who ever lived were Christians—people who discovered laws of nature or the inner workings of biology or helped us make greater sense of ancient history. But there's no guarantee in Christianity of being smarter than anybody else.

A lot of the people who've helped us most with the deep questions of science and nature weren't Christians at all. Some of them didn't even believe in God. So Christians have no major advantage when it comes to intelligence.

But Christians are at a great advantage when it comes to the wisdom from on high. We have access by faith to the deepest secret of the universe: God is true and his word and work are made manifest through the person of Jesus Christ, his Son.

This is why the best advice on how to manage life usually doesn't come from our know-it-all, bookworm cousins but from our seen-it-all, Bible-reading grandmas.

Oh, sure, it's great to read a lot and study a lot and know a lot of stuff. But it's far more important to know the right *person*.

Now, to be clear, part of pursuing the life of faith is getting to know more, especially knowing more of the Bible and what it tells us about God and his ways. Part of the Great Commandment is to love the Lord your God with "all your mind" (Matthew 22:37). But the apostle Paul tells us in 1 Corinthians 13:2, that if we understand all knowledge but don't have love, we actually have nothing. (In fact, he says we *are* nothing.)

Today's gift is a reminder that in the gift of Jesus we get the gift of wisdom. Jesus is in fact wisdom personified. He is the perfect embodiment not just of God, who is omniscient, but also of the sinless man, who is fully in line with the will of God. And when we receive the gift of Christ, we receive the Spirit of this wisdom too. The Holy Spirit comes into our life. The wisdom he brings to us begins with a holy reverence for God (Psalm 111:10). He convicts us of sin and helps us turn away from evil, which is also wisdom (Job 28:28). Jesus promises us that the Holy Spirit will guide us into all truth (John 16:13).

None of this is something we can do apart from the Spirit of Jesus. All the treasures of wisdom and knowledge, Paul says in Colossians 2:3, are hidden in him.

In the gospel, then, we receive by grace the kind of wisdom that makes the difference between light and darkness, life and death, joy and despair. You may get some books for Christmas that promise to improve your

IQ. You may get some games or tools that challenge your problem-solving skills. But today open up an appreciation of the wisdom of Christ. It is given to us to help us see into the very secret things of the world—to know true wisdom, which surpasses all earthly know-how.

If you know Jesus, you know the true wisdom of the ages.

13. His Gospel
Is Peace

Today's Gift: Contentment

"But godliness with contentment is great gain."
—*1 Timothy 6:6*

There are innumerable obstacles to contentment during the holidays, but the biggest is probably our persistent desire to *consume*. That's counterintuitive, I know, because we figure the more we get, the more we will be satisfied. But just think of how that works at Christmas dinner. The more I stuff myself with my wife's delicious beef Wellington and spicy mashed potatoes, the more miserable I feel afterwards. The problem is not with the food but with the way I'm consuming it.

The same is true for our gift exchanges. The Christmas holidays don't introduce consumerism to our culture; they just dress it up. Every year, we go bigger and better, trying to outdo ourselves—and each other—and every year, we wonder why we're still not entirely satisfied.

Envy can drive some of our discontentment too. Some of us are still trying to "keep up with the Joneses." If a neighbor or family member got a cool new gadget, we've got to have one too—preferably a newer and shinier model. Every commercial we see holds out the promise of a perfect holiday gift-giving experience; that bracelet, that tablet, that shiny new car with the gigantic red bow on it. (Where exactly does one buy gigantic red bows, anyway?)

But sometimes it's not envy over stuff that drives our consumeristic discontent at all. Sometimes it's our envy over experiences or relationships. Maybe we're jealous that the kids are taking our grandchildren to the other grandparents this year. Maybe we're jealous that our sibling is announcing their engagement while we're still single, or they're pregnant while we're still struggling with infertility. Maybe we're jealous that the church across the way is conducting more services with far more people while we're still holding that same pitiful Christmas Eve candlelight reflection that fewer people attend every year.

Whatever your situation, you have an opportunity for envy and thus an opportunity for discontentment. The key to contentment, then, is to remember, in the midst of all that we lack this year, all that we've *already been given!*

You know that when Jesus was born, he was not born into a life of wealth and privilege. It does not seem as though Jesus was born into an earthly family that had many advantages or many opportunities to keep up with whoever were Nazareth's version of the Joneses. You know that the Son of God, in fact, surrendered his privileges as the heavenly King to enter the world as the humble son of a carpenter. And yet he held within himself all the riches of righteousness and glory. That poor baby Jesus, crying in the bed of straw in a barn rank with dirty livestock, was in fact the richest person in the universe.

There is a beautiful truth in this juxtaposition for us. It is imperative to remember—as the happy bells of consumerism ring all around us in the streets, on the radio, on our screens, and sometimes even in our churches—that because of Christ, everything we need *we already have.*

Paul tells his young protégé that godliness with contentment is great gain (1 Timothy 6:6). What does he mean? In context, he has just warned Timothy about false teaching and the people who fall prey to it. This vulnerability comes not just from doctrinal immaturity but from a kind of emotional or spiritual immaturity as well. Paul tells Timothy that there are people who give way to envy in their lives because they imagine that spiritual superiority comes from material gain. It's another kind of prosperity gospel thinking; it's the kind that reasons that having more and more stuff is a sign of God's favor and, ultimately, the true source of finally being satisfied.

But for emotionally immature people like this, there is never enough. Enough is always envisioned as "a little bit more." It never ends. The discontent never goes away.

The only truly great gain is godliness. And godliness brings with it contentment because godliness connects us to the endless storehouse of God, who always satisfies, rather than the decaying riches of the world, which never can.

Here's what to do during these holidays that always promise peace while simultaneously stealing it from us: look up. Take your eyes off of what other people have that you might want. Take your eyes off of earthly situations or rewards that are constantly passing away. Lift your eyes to the heavens. Follow the north star of the gospel to the center of its glory, the gift of Jesus Christ himself. Through faith in him, you receive his redemption and his riches. He gives you, by faith, a declaration of godliness in the imputation of his righteousness and a commitment to your godliness in the indwelling presence of his Spirit. There is no gift that could be greater. If you've gained this gift, you have a rock-solid, never-shifting, "forever and for always" foundation of heart-filled contentment.

14. Join the Triumph of the Skies

Today's Gift: Victory

"He disarmed the rulers and authorities and put them to open shame, by triumphing over them in him."—Colossians 2:15

One of my favorite traditions over the Christmas holidays is watching football on the weekends with my wife. She and I both really enjoy the NFL, and since I'm usually traveling a lot during the fall months, it's part of our holiday rest to get home from church on Sundays in December, put on a big pot of chili, change into comfy clothes, and snuggle up on the couch to watch the big games. The NFL's regular season is winding down at this point, as teams jockey for position and a shot at the playoffs, so our greatest football recreation comes from the players' hardest push toward finishing with a winning record.

I confess that, sometimes, these games are not as relaxing for me as I expect them to be. When my team is not doing well, I get pretty animated. I'll yell at the screen, wave my hands, and very often stand up and approach the television, as if my proximity to it might somehow electronically affect the abilities of the players. When my team *is* doing well, I'm even more animated! I jump up, I shout, I dance around.

When the New England Patriots dramatically won Super Bowl 49 against the Seattle Seahawks thanks to a last-second goal-line interception, I actually broke a chair in celebration at the party we were attending to watch it. When my favorite player of all time, Tom Brady, led those same Patriots in Super Bowl 51 on a miraculous comeback against a 25-point deficit to the Atlanta Falcons to win in overtime—maybe the greatest game in Super Bowl history—I nearly passed out.

When our team loses, we feel the loss in our guts. When our team wins—especially when it's a spectacular, against-all-odds kind of win—we feel that too, dramatically so. We feel it despite the fact that we haven't done anything to help the cause. Similar to the teaching of the imputation of Christ's righteousness—in which the perfect obedience is graciously credited to our account as if we'd earned it ourselves—the vicarious triumph of the Christian is accomplished through a victory we've contributed nothing to!

Spiritually speaking, we are dead in our sins. We certainly don't have the weapons, much less the ability, to defeat the forces of wickedness arrayed against us. We do not have the power to conquer the sin and death that hold us captive. Metaphorically speaking, we are drooling idiots watching from the couch.

Do you remember the story of David and Goliath? I don't know if violent battles like the one confronting the Israelites in the assembled might of Philistines quite qualify as ancient sports, but there is certainly a similar vibe in the idea of sending out representatives to fight so we don't have to. The Philistines make this offer: *Send out your best warrior; we'll send out ours. The winner will win for his side.* They have a ringer lined up: Goliath. But so do the Israelites. Only, they don't know it.

Eventually David goes on to face Goliath, and you know how that story ends—with a giant severed head hanging from David's little hand. The Israelites win! They didn't do anything to secure that win, but nevertheless win they did. And the ensuing story shows us the Israelites plundering the Philistines' camp, enjoying the spoils of the victory to which they contributed nothing.

That's you and me. We cannot overcome the gigantic enemies we face. Sin is too infectious. Death is too powerful. The devil is too shrewd. We do not stand a chance.

"Send out your best," they taunt, and we can't even lift ourselves off the couch.

But we've got a ringer we didn't expect. He enters the stadium as a naked baby. He doesn't look like much. He doesn't seem to come from much. He doesn't seem to carry much. And when he's introduced to the spectators, he's on a donkey, greeted with waving palm branches. (Shouldn't he have a sword?) Our stomach begins to sink. Maybe there's no hope.

And then round by round, quarter by quarter—however you measure this competition—it's basically no competition at all! David scooped up five stones, but only needed one. Jesus defeats the devil in the wilderness, rebuffing all his attacks. He withstands the allures of the flesh thereafter. And in the final, climactic moments, when the enemy thinks he might actually win, the devil is overcome in the greatest, fateful sucker punch ever devised. At the cross, "[Christ] disarmed the rulers and authorities and put them to open shame, by triumphed over them in him" (Colossians 2:15). And at his resurrection, he triumphs over the grave and death itself, securing the keys to both.

The knot in our stomach instantly unties. Our held breath releases. We shout. We cry. We nearly pass out. The victory is achieved—not by us, but it's ours nevertheless!

This is what Christmas can be about, if we have the heart to discern it. In our hustling and bustling over the coming week, let us never forget that all of the wonderful beauty of our holiday celebrations are merely symbols of the spoils of victory achieved by Jesus and given to us in a ransacking of the enemy's camp. We too get to conquer sin, death, and the grave—even from the comfort of our Christmas couch.

"Thanks be to God, who gives us the victory through our Lord Jesus Christ."
(1 Corinthians 15:57)

15. O Hush the Noise,
Ye Men of Strife

Today's Gift: Rest

*"So then, there remains a Sabbath rest for the
people of God."—Hebrews 4:9*

Tired yet?

It's just ten days until Christmas, so it's probably a good time to go ahead and open up the gift of rest today. You might need it.

I tend to think that over all the preparations for the holidays most people resemble one of two people. We're either a Martha or a Mary.

If you're not familiar with what I mean, let me remind you of this scene from Luke 10:

> *"Now as they went on their way, Jesus entered a village. And a woman named Martha welcomed him into her house. And she had a sister called Mary, who sat at the Lord's feet and listened to his teaching. But Martha was distracted with much serving. And she went up to him and said, 'Lord, do you not care that my sister has left me to serve alone? Tell her then to help me.' But the*

> *Lord answered her, 'Martha, Martha, you are anxious and troubled about many things, but one thing is necessary. Mary has chosen the good portion, which will not be taken away from her.'" (v 38-42)*

It may seem noble to always be working, or it may seem impressive. Do you see yourself in that scene? Are you Martha? Or Mary?

Marthas are running themselves ragged about now, overscheduling themselves and everyone around them. They've got spreadsheets upon spreadsheets set up to tell them what gifts to buy, what food to prepare, what parties to attend, what projects to finish, and so on and so forth. Marthas are the ones who get to the end of the Christmas holidays and feel exhausted; they need vacations from their vacations.

There's nothing wrong with being busy, of course. Most of us can't avoid it anyway. But there is a particular problem with the biblical Martha's kind of busy-ness. Her busyness was a distraction from Jesus. This is a very real danger at this time of year, when we are so wrapped up in "doing Christmas stuff"; we actually get distracted from the point of it all. "Martha, Martha," Jesus sighs...

Are you anxious right now?

You know, sometimes our failure to keep the Sabbath and our addiction to busyness are not about liking work too much but about not liking being still. Maybe staying busy has become a reliable distraction for you from the pain of your life. "If I'm still," you think, "I'll have to face the stuff inside my head and heart that I don't want to face. I'll have to struggle with the trauma of my past or the pain of my present."

But a refusal to be still doesn't just allow us to avoid facing difficult things; it stops us presenting those difficult things to Jesus. Between busying yourself as a distraction from your pain or being still to sit at the feet of Jesus, choose the better portion, which is Jesus.

Jesus is the point of Christmas, of course, but he's also the point of the rest we can celebrate at this time of year too. Jesus is the point of the Sabbath rest, given to believers not as a burdensome commandment but as a gift. You see, observing a Sabbath rest is ultimately about the rest we receive when we come to faith in Christ. In fact, one of the passages where we see the command to keep the Sabbath actually reflects the concept of freedom from work.

Deuteronomy 5:15 gives us a significant reason to observe the Sabbath: the Israelites are told to observe the Sabbath so that they might remember their freedom from slavery:

> "You shall remember that you were a slave in the land of Egypt, and the LORD your God brought you out from there with a mighty hand and an outstretched arm. Therefore the LORD your God commanded you to keep the Sabbath day."

The reason stated there for why the law was given is to remind the Israelites of freedom! Sabbath is a reminder of the rest we now enjoy from enslavement to sin, thanks to the saving grace of God.

The author of Hebrews writes:

> *"So then, there remains a Sabbath rest for the people of God, for whoever has entered God's rest has also rested from his works as God did from his. Let us therefore strive to enter that rest." (4:9-11)*

Why must we *strive* to enter that *rest*? Because our hearts are bent toward the flesh. Our flesh yearns for works righteousness. We want to believe we are self-made people. And we like the idea of being rewarded for our accomplishments, real or imagined. So part of the process of abiding with God every day is pressing "reset" to the gospel in our hearts and minds.

Are we still obligated to obey God? Yes, but not as a means of earning or meriting what he's done for us, but as a worshipful gratitude for what he's given to us freely in Jesus.

Jesus did not cry out from the cross *Get to work*, but "It is finished" (John 19:30). He did not say, "Come to me all who are weary and heavy laden, and I will give you..." *steps*. He said, "Come to me ... and I will give you rest" (Matthew 11:28).

Rest is another wonderful gift of grace.

Are you trying to earn your way to rest? Earn your way to heaven? Earn your way to right standing with God? You don't have to. You can't. God loves sinners so much that he sent Jesus to live, die, and rise again so that we might be free from sin, free from the law that pronounces condemnation, and free from the bondage of self-righteousness and works religion. If you want to be truly free, only the Son can make that happen. And if you want his grace, you can have it. Come and take a load off in the presence of the Lord who loves you.

The Christmas to-do list can wait. He will give you rest.

16. Adam's Likeness Now Efface; Stamp Thine Image in Its Place

Today's Gift: Sanctification

"And we all, with unveiled face, beholding the glory of the Lord, are being transformed into the same image from one degree of glory to another. For this comes from the Lord who is the Spirit."—2 Corinthians 3:18

Can I tell you about one of the best gifts I ever got? It was a birthday present, not a Christmas present, but my birthday's in November, so that's close enough. As I told you in the devotion from the day before yesterday, I'm a big fan of the New England Patriots football team, and that's due in large part because I'm a big fan of their long-time champion quarterback Tom Brady. But even though we'd lived in New England for a number of years, I was never able to go to a game. For one thing, we lived in Vermont, about four hours away from the Patriots' home games in Foxboro, Massachusetts. But mainly, I just couldn't afford it. I drove out to the facilities to attend the team's training camp a couple of times, but I had to be content with being a fan who never saw a game live.

A few years ago, after we'd moved to Kansas City, my oldest daughter Macy was living in Pennsylvania for college, and she cooked up a scheme to rectify this injustice. And she and the rest of my family were pretty clever about the whole thing. They told me that my birthday present was going to be to fly to Pennsylvania and watch the game (on TV) with Macy at a friend's house. The story was that as the lone Patriots fan among her friends, Macy was tired of being the only person rooting for them during the games. (The real importance of this gift for me, of course, was to get to see my daughter, whom I missed very much. Because of course I could have watched the game on my TV at home.)

In any event, I was grateful to be able to see Macy. So I traveled with my wife and younger daughter out to Pennsylvania one chilly November weekend, and the first thing we did was take Macy out to a nice dinner. "There's more to your birthday gift," Macy said, and she handed me a broad, flat gift tidily wrapped in festive paper. I opened it to discover a scrapbook. It appeared to be a tribute to my fandom for Tom Brady. I thought that was pretty cute. But when I opened the book, I discovered I'd been "had."

My gift was not a trip to Pennsylvania to watch the Patriots game on TV with Macy and her friends. Macy had in fact enlisted the help of many of our family friends to cover the cost of four tickets for our whole family to attend the game in Philadelphia, as the Patriots played the Eagles. I was going to get to see Tom Brady play live for the very first time.

What began as a neat gift got bigger and bigger, until it actually blew me away with something I could not have anticipated—something I had hoped for for a long time, but I had honestly kind of given up hope it would ever happen.

The bigness of the gospel is like that. This is part of the idea behind this entire book, of course. Every day, we open up another of the many gifts we receive in the one gospel, and thereby we are rediscovering just how gracious God is. Today's gift demonstrates this surprising bigness too. Because most people who think about sanctification—the process by which Christians become holy—think mainly about their efforts and their contributions to the process. Now, to be clear, the work of sanctification certainly entails our obedient pursuit of personal holiness. But the Bible speaks of sanctification as a gift to be received, as well. Does that surprise you?

In 1 Corinthians 15:1-2, the apostle Paul briefly outlines the power of the gospel in a really surprising way. First, he refers to believers having "received" (past tense) that gospel. This refers to the experience of conversion: that moment when one who is an unbeliever exercises saving faith in Jesus Christ. They pass from darkness to light, from death to life. They "get saved."

This is what most of us think of when we think of the gift of the gospel. It is a gift for lost people by which they can be found. And it *is* that, of course. But Paul doesn't stop there. The gift gets bigger.

Next he says that Christians "stand" (present tense) in the gospel. I take Paul to mean here the imputation of Christ's righteousness (which we examined a few days ago). By the grace of God, sinners don't just get forgiven; they also become clothed in the obedience of Christ. This too is what it means to be justified by faith.

But wait—there's more!

Just as I opened that scrapbook and got blown away by the enormity of a gift that I already thought was a pretty big deal to start with, we turn the page of the gospel story and see that Paul says that those who "received" the gospel and who "stand" in the gospel are also "being saved" (present future tense) by the gospel. I believe the apostle is here referring to the work of sanctification. And the implications of this are staggering, because it means that, ultimately, our ability to become holy isn't powered by our own efforts at spirituality or religiosity but by the finished work of Jesus Christ. Sanctification is a glorious gift of grace.

It helps, too, to remember what the point of sanctification is. To become more holy in our thoughts and actions is not about becoming more impressive to others. Still less is it about being able to impress God! Sanctification is not about superiority. It's about becoming more like the Jesus who saved us.

This is what it means to become more holy: to be conformed more to the image of Christ. And Paul says in 1 Corinthians 15:2 that says this work is accomplished by the gospel. In 2 Corinthians 3:18, he reiterates this same idea but in a way that is perhaps more startling: it's by "beholding the glory of the Lord" that we "are being transformed into the same image." In other words, there is something about being exposed to the glory of Jesus that begins to change us more into the likeness of Jesus. In other words, beholding is a kind of becoming.

If we want to be more like Jesus, we have to look more *to* Jesus. We can't expect a vague "Christmas spirit" to produce genuine kindness, gentleness, goodness, and the rest of that Christ-like spiritual fruit in us. We must look to Jesus.

And the promise is that if we will commit to centering on the gospel, commit to "fixing our eyes on Jesus" (Hebrews 12:2 NIV), the Holy Spirit will grow the gift of grace supernaturally in our lives. Over time, we who look to Jesus more and more will begin to look like Jesus more and more.

The gift of the gospel is bigger than we expected, isn't it?

17. Take Us to Heaven to Live with Thee There

Today's Gift: Glorification

"Behold! I tell you a mystery. We shall not all sleep, but we shall all be changed."
—1 Corinthians 15:51

In C.S. Lewis's children's novel *The Lion, the Witch, and the Wardrobe*, the world of Narnia lies under the cursed spell of the White Witch. The primary effect of this spell is that in the land it is always winter, never Christmas. The land lies perennially covered in snow and ice.

But then something happens; the tide begins to turn. The four Pevensie children, who have found their way through the enchanted wardrobe from their world into the world of Narnia, are greeted at one point by Father Christmas (Santa Claus), who distributes to each of them a personal gift. Each gift, as it turns out, will be instrumental in the victory of Aslan the Lion over the White Witch and the liberation of Narnia from her spell.

The arrival of Father Christmas is a major turning point on the way to this victory. For if a kind of Christmas can be celebrated in a land that has only known the cold of winter without its joys, something must be changing. The return of Christmas gifts is the first sign that a great thaw is taking place. "Aslan is on the move," Father Christmas says. "The Witch's magic is weakening."

This is all Lewis's way, of course, of representing what was beginning to happen at the point of the incarnation. On Christmas Day we will celebrate the day when the curse began to crumble, because on the day Jesus was born, this divine life of heaven invading the stuff of earth was the first signal to the power of sin and death that redemption was afoot. And it is his arrival that signals the beginning of the end of death!

Yesterday we reflected on the gracious gift of sanctification. This is the process by which the Holy Spirit conforms us more and more to the image of Christ. This is a process that, by grace, we participate in. We are active in our pursuit of holiness. But we are "working out" what the Spirit has worked in us (Philippians 2:12-13; Colossians 1:29). This means that our sanctification is just as much founded on and empowered by grace as is our justification.

But the gifts don't stop there. Imagine if after opening that scrapbook to learn I was going to go to an actual game to see my favorite athlete play football, that I turned another page to learn that in fact I was going to get to meet him after the game. If I woke up tomorrow morning with my head sewn to the carpet, I don't think I would be more surprised! The gifts of the gospel keep coming too.

For instance, in Romans 8:30, Paul presents to believers what is often today called the Golden Chain of Salvation: "And those whom he predestined he also called, and those whom he called he also justified, and those whom he justified he also glorified." Each entailment of the gospel in this chain builds on the previous one. Our salvation by grace begins with God's predestining purposes before time began, held only in the eternal mind of his ageless and changeless self. Because of these predestining purposes, he then calls sinners to himself. The effectual call is followed by justification (and all that justification entails). Justification is then the entry point to the spiritual work of sanctification—implied in Romans 8:30—which culminates in the climactic link in the chain: glorification.

If sanctification is the process by which we become more like Jesus, glorification is the conclusion of that process, at which point we finally enjoy a sinless, deathless new heavens and new earth with immortal resurrection bodies that are like Jesus' immortal resurrection body. Glorification begins for us the moment we begin enjoying the eternality of the restoration of all things.

In Romans 8:30, Paul refers to glorification in the past tense ("he also glorified"), despite the fact that it is still an unrealized reality. I think he does so for a couple of reasons. First, there is a sense in which, spiritually speaking, we have been glorified in that we are united to Christ, having been buried with him and having risen with him and having been seated with him in the heavenly places. It is reflective of the Christian's present union with Christ, who is himself seated at the right hand of the Father in glory. Secondly I think Paul speaks of glorification in Romans 8:30 in the past tense to remind us that the promise of glorification is sure. This is a way for the apostle to indicate that the spiritual reality of our glorification is settled by the finished work of Christ and will remain unthreatened. As Jesus says to his disciples, *Where I am you will be also* (John 14:3). You can bank on it.

So when Jesus is born, he is the first sinless man since Adam. But, unlike Adam, this sinless man is never to fall. He is the second Adam and the last we will need. And as Jesus grows in wisdom and stature, following perfectly the will of the Father, he commences at adulthood a public ministry that is less about teaching people a new religion and more about ushering in a new kingdom. The kingdom of heaven is at hand in and through Jesus, and everywhere he goes, he is signaling to the curse, and to those who suffer under it, that its day is drawing to an end.

In his parables, he gives pictures of a world set to rights and unfallenness again. In his miracles, he does the same, showing not just his divine power over creation but his intention eventually to re-create creation itself and restore it to a better state even than unfallen Eden. And his concluding miraculous triumphs are, of course, his own resurrection and ascension. These bring the promise to those who repent and follow him that we too will be raised from the dead; we tool will ascend into the heavenly place. "Behold! I tell you a mystery," Paul writes in 1 Corinthians 15:51. "We shall not all sleep, but we shall all be changed."

And when Jesus returns to earth, we will return with him—sons of glory riding in the blazing trail of the glorious Son.

The promise of glorification is the promise of becoming the me I should have always been but cannot in my own power become. It is the promise of getting there not by the exaltation of myself but by the exaltation of the one who reigns over and inside of me. The promise of glorification is the promise of becoming like the one I should always have been like. One day, I will finally be my sinless self because, one day, I will finally be fully conformed to the likeness of Jesus.

The Christmas story holds the promise of glorification out to us because it tells us that God took on our image, that we might someday take on his. We will reflect him beautifully and eternally on a new earth restored according to his glory.

It's getting close. Can you feel it? Aslan is on the move. Christmas is coming.

18. In His Name, All Oppression Shall Cease

Today's Gift: Justice/Vindication

*"He has brought down the mighty from their
thrones and exalted those of humble estate."*
—Luke 1:52

A lot of us hold our musical tastes very dear, don't we? And our opinions extend not just to our must-repeat favorite Christmas songs; they also extend to those Christmas songs we just can't stand!

One song that seems to spark intense debate every Christmas season is Mark Lowry's "Mary, Did You Know?" Sincere believers bicker back and forth about whether the song is profound or profoundly naïve. I'll admit it's not one of my favorite Christmas songs, but I don't understand the ire many hold for it. Some of the arguments center on its central idea—that Jesus' mother wasn't fully aware of the divinity of the son to whom she was going to give birth. (I happen to think Mary did know she was giving birth to the Son of God, but I still think the song is on the right track to suggest she might not have known all the implications of that.)

In the song, the narrator is asking Mary a series of questions that pertain to the Messiah's power. "Did you know he'll walk on water? Did you know he'll heal?" That kind of thing. It's a fine conceit, as far as it goes, but the truth is, we do have a much older song that tells us much of the extent that Mary knew about the Messiah she was carrying. It comes from Mary herself.

In Luke 1, as Mary is visiting with her relative Elizabeth, she is moved over the prophetic promise of bearing the Christ-child to sing a little prayer we today call The Magnificat. One thing I notice in this song is that Mary does indeed expect her son to be powerful, but her focus is less on miraculous feats and more on merciful deeds. In other words, she's not inordinately concerned with whether Jesus can miraculously fill an empty table (though of course he can, and *did* numerous times), but whether in fact he might turn that table over. In other words, Mary's song seems to run in the long line of Old Testament messianic expectation toward *justice*.

> *"He has shown strength with his arm;*
>   *he has scattered the proud in the thoughts of*
>   *their hearts;*
>   *he has brought down the mighty from their*
>   *thrones*
>   *and exalted those of humble estate;*
>   *he has filled the hungry with good things,*
>   *and the rich he has sent away empty."*
>   *(Luke 1:51-53)*

The portrait of the coming Messiah in this song is one of rescue and restoration. Mary is expecting her son to bring about the vindication of those who've been on the outside all their lives, to the marginalized, and the exploited. She is expecting that in the victory of the one true King, there will finally be justice enacted in our fallen world.

This is certainly something we all look forward to today, isn't it?

We find ourselves currently in a strange cultural moment, where multitudes of chickens are coming home to roost. Victims of abuse bravely and boldly exposing the perpetrators of their abuse and in many cases also exposing widespread systemic and institutional injustice in handling the aftermath. Even the evangelical church has not been immune to both incidents of abuse and institutional mishandling of the aftermath.

And unfortunately what often rises to the surface in the Christian's understanding of these matters is a superficial understanding of the complexities of pain, shame, pathology, even injustice. A sentimental theology will not do here. "Let go and let God" will not do.

And when speaking to victims—whether of abuse or any other number of less traumatic yet still painful sins—we cannot represent Christianity as a Band-Aid. The cross of Jesus is simultaneously a place of immense grace and a place of immense wrath. It is a place of excruciating pain but also exhilarating promise.

And so we ought to ask ourselves: What does the coming of Jesus mean to those who have been sinned against, to those who have been recipients up till now of justice delayed or denied?

In Mary's song, the Messiah has the power. He has the power to destroy the strongholds and liberate those imprisoned in them. So while the gospel warns against equating our sense of identity with a kind of victim-hood, it is also realistic and honest about the injustice perpetrated against so many of us. Mary does not shy away from the subject of injustice like so many evangel-icals today. We are tired of conflict around this issue, so we avoid it or accommodate "theologies of glory" that deny the importance of it altogether. But the cross of Christ in particular reminds us that the pain of injus-tice is real while *at the same time* reminding us that the promise of justice is sure.

The cross shows the full gravity, the full scandal, the full evil of the terrible things sinners can do, not just to Jesus but also to each other. The gospel announces the forgiveness of sin but not the whitewashing of it!

I think of Joseph forgiving his brothers: "What you meant for evil, God meant for good" (Genesis 50:20). He is forgiving them, yes, and he's acknowledging that God has a purpose for his own pain—that all things work together for the good of those who love God (Romans 8:28)—but he's not saying "It's all right." He says it plainly: "You meant it for evil."

Similarly, the cross brings stark clarity to the world. Sin is real. Injustice is real.

Thus, the Messiah's work on the cross (and out of the empty tomb!) carry the promise that our pain, our exploitation, our victimization will be compensated for. Through the cross, victims will become victors.

Hear this, those of you who are hurting: God has not thrown you away. He has not forgotten you. He will plead your case. He will redeem the time you spend in pain.

Consider Psalm 126:5-6:

> *"Those who sow in tears*
> *shall reap with shouts of joy!*
> *He who goes out weeping,*
> *bearing the seed for sowing,*
> *shall come home with shouts of joy."*

Consider Isaiah 61:2-3, which says that when the day of the Lord comes, God will come:

> *"... to comfort all who mourn;*
> *to grant to those who mourn in Zion—*
> *to give them a beautiful headdress*
> *instead of ashes,*
> *the oil of gladness*
> *instead of mourning,*
> *the garment of praise instead of a faint spirit."*

Consider Jesus beginning his Sermon on the Mount with these declarations:

> *"Blessed are the poor in spirit,*
> *for theirs is the kingdom of heaven.*

> *Blessed are those who mourn,*
> *for they shall be comforted.*
> *Blessed are the meek,*
> *for they shall inherit the earth."*
>
> *(Matthew 5:3-5)*

You Christians who hurt and wait, hurt and wait, hurt and wait, your day is coming. Habakkuk 2:3 says, "If it seems slow, wait for it; it will surely come; it will not delay."

The cross (and the resurrection) mean you aren't just validated but vindicated. The cross of Christ ensures that your cause will be taken up and justice will prevail.

The cross is God's promise that justice delayed will not be justice denied.

There is a reckoning coming! Justice will be done. Mary's song says so.

So, yeah, she knew.

19. Free Thine Own from Satan's Tyranny

Today's Gift: Freedom

*Now the Lord is the Spirit, and where the Spirit
of the Lord is, there is freedom."*
—2 Corinthians 3:17

My wife and I have a favorite Christmas movie: *Mickey's Once upon a Christmas*. It's a lesser-known direct-to-DVD Disney feature that we enjoyed with our girls when they were little that we now watch every year without them. The movie assembles three short animated stories tied together with the common theme of love for family. The first story, "Stuck on Christmas," tells the tale of Donald Duck's nephews Huey, Dewey, and Louie, who, at the end of a rather exhilarating Christmas Day, send out a bedtime prayer-like wish that every day could be Christmas. It seems like a brilliant idea at the time. Why shouldn't every day be like Christmas Day?

Well, the precocious ducklings soon find out. Their wish comes true, and they are trapped in a Groundhog Day-like cycle of neverending visits from overbearing family, angry scolding from Uncle Donald, gluttonous overeating at dinner, and the general malaise that sets in when anything good becomes a monotonous drudgery. The joy of reliving the same wonderful day soon gives way to the boredom of going through the motions.

What they discover, of course, is that their self-interested rush through a special day has also taken a serious toll on those around them, including their beloved Uncle Donald. The care he has put into providing presents and food and a warm, loving home for his nephews has been ignored and squandered. Eventually the boys are overcome with guilt and realize that the endless repetition of Christmas Day will finally end if they finally do it right. And so they do. They are patient and thankful toward their uncle. They are loving and kind to their visiting relatives. They are generous with their gifts. And soon enough, they are set free from the tyranny of the good thing.

You know I'm about to turn this into a spiritual illustration, right? Well, I am. But with a twist.

First of all, as silly and juvenile as this Disney movie is, and as much as my wife's and my devotion to it is driven largely out of sentimentality, there is definitely something in this first story that resonates with me. I am a glutton for too much of a good thing. I frequently do not know when to say "when." And I also love Christmas. I kind of wish it would never end. But I realize that my desires in these areas have more to do with self-indulgence than they do with any kind of opportunity for service or generosity.

What this sappy little cartoon does pretty well, actually, is illustrate the bondage of idolatry. See, idols aren't just bad things that we exalt in our lives. I grew up in a church culture that, when warning against idols, usually mentioned things like alcohol or drugs or (for us kids) TV watching. But I don't remember anybody ever saying to me that my family could be an idol. That work could be an idol. That my marriage could be an idol. That even my Christian life or my ministry could be an idol. But I have been much more susceptible over the years to making idols out of those good things than the few "bad" things I was warned about. Like those stupid little ducks, I have assumed that deriving my greatest joy from earthly things would satisfy, but it has only left me discouraged, depressed, and, in some situations, in despair.

There can be such a thing as too much of a good thing. Especially when we are expecting good things to fulfill us the way only God can.

Is this a danger for you this Christmas? Are you expecting the celebrations, the family visits, the music and the movies, and the mountains of gifts to stir something in you, change you, or meet your needs for acceptance, joy, and peace? This is a losing game. It's the kind of thing where what looks like a party is really enslavement. Because any time we ascribe ultimate worth to created things rather than the Creator himself, we fall prey to the bondage of idols.

In the Disney movie, Huey, Dewey, and Louie undo their prison of time by learning how to be good little boys. It's similar to the predicament faced by Bill Murray's character in *Groundhog Day*; he can get out of the endless cycle of mundane life in Punxsutawney by finally becoming a good person—finally caring for others more than himself. It's a sweet morality tale, but it bears no resemblance to spiritual reality as the Bible tells it.

No, according to God's word, we are dead in our sins, enslaved to the flesh, and imprisoned in our false worship. We cannot get out of the prison of idolatry on our own. We can't become good people on our own. We need a liberator. We need an external power to set us free. Until then, our situation is hopeless.

Praise God that King Jesus is a liberator of the captives! He has come to set us free from all that enslaves us, including our devilish devotion to idols. And when we receive Christ Jesus, his Spirit takes up residence in our hearts, implanting the power of freedom in us to resist temptation, repent of sin, and reject the shiny wares of rival gods in the world. Paul writes, "Now the Lord is the Spirit, and where the Spirit of the Lord is, there is freedom" (2 Corinthians 3:17).

This Christmas, don't get wrapped up in the idea that more of this earthly stuff can suffice for what it is pointing to. It's well and good to celebrate all the good things God in his common grace has given us. Love your family, enjoy good food, dance to good music, laugh at good movies. Do Christmas right! But don't get so wrapped up that you forget the point of it all—the special grace of Jesus. In his kingdom, we can finally escape the cycles of sin and shame and worthless objects of worship. "If the Son sets you free, you will be free indeed" (John 8:36).

20. Why Lies He in Such Mean Estate?

Today's Gift: Priesthood

"But you are a chosen race, a royal priesthood, a holy nation, a people for his own possession, that you may proclaim the excellencies of him who called you out of darkness into his marvelous light."—1 Peter 2:9

Everything about who we are has changed because of the first Christmas. The entrance of the God of the universe into frail human flesh has begun a complete undoing of earthly business as usual. The Lord of all creation has invited himself into the world he has made so that anyone who might find room for him in their hearts might become a new creation themselves (2 Corinthians 5:17).

By the gospel, sinners become saints. Dead souls spring to life. Objects of wrath become objects of mercy. The poor in Christ become rich. The slave in Christ becomes free. The profane in Christ become... holy. And this is all because the only one of us who absolutely does not deserve the worse of all those contrasts (and others) willingly took those unwanted characteristics upon himself.

Ponder your nativity set. I bet you have one set up somewhere. On your mantle or coffee table. Maybe it's on the TV stand or desk. Ours sits high above our living room on the sill of a tall picture window overlooking the field behind our house. It's nothing fancy. I think we got it at a Hobby Lobby store. It consists of a simple wooden hut made of gray-painted wood, tufted inside with fake straw. The figures inside are simple, not ornate. The whole thing probably cost a couple of bucks to make—I probably don't want to know where. It cost us all of about 15 dollars. It's not the kind of thing that would catch your eye. And that's kind of the point, I think.

We place it about nine feet (2.7m) off the floor of our living room so that we'd have to intentionally look for it to see it, and then have to crane our necks up in the process. This too is a reminder to me that focusing on the humble birth of our splendorous King is something I will have to be intentional about. It's hard enough throughout the year to remember that my Christ came in a humble and lowly way. It's especially difficult at Christmas.

Isn't that ironic? The time of year when we ought to be focusing on the humility of Jesus is filled with garlands and tinsel, lights and color, feasting and excess of all kinds. And there the little baby Jesus sits in his fragile wooden creche, staring wanly out at a pale sea of hay.

Let us never forget.

And let us never forget why he did it. The King did not initially come as a warrior on a steed but as a baby among donkeys. The divine Prophet did not come to a ready-made megachurch crowd but to a handful of shepherds. Our interceding Priest did not come in a majestic robe to slaughter his sacrifices for us but as a lowly mediator swaddled among the very livestock which, back then, would be slaughtered for the sins of the people. Indeed, he came to be the sacrificial Lamb himself. And he did all of this for us.

He did it for us. He came to this lowly estate that our estate might be raised.

I love the way W. Chatterton Dix put it in his classic Christmas carol, "What Child Is This?":

Why lies He in such mean estate
Where ox and ass are feeding?
Good Christian, fear: for sinners here
The silent Word is pleading.

Reflecting on the humble entrance into the world of our Priest-King Jesus, we sing in this song about the inscrutable irony of the incarnation. The Christ child came as the least of us, but he was undoubtedly the best.

In Hebrews 7, we find a lengthy excursus about how Jesus is the fulfillment of the Israelite priesthood: how he stands as a priest forever according to the order of Melchizedek. He has done this ultimately to become the priest according to a better covenant than the one the patriarchs lived under. He comes as the guarantor of the covenant of grace.

And under the covenant of grace, something extraordinary happens. In the ancient days of the prior covenantal system, only certain men of a certain lineage could function as priests. But when Christ comes, announcing the kingdom is finally "at hand," that indeed, it can even be found within the hearts of those who trust in him, he expands the priesthood in his name to anyone who believes in him. He makes us all the redeemed, actually priests ourselves! The apostle Peter tells us that Jesus has made us "a royal priesthood" (1 Peter 2:9).

No longer do we need the ongoing work of sacrifices conducted by elite third parties. Jesus has put an end to the sacrifices by the sacrifice of himself. And as our final and everlasting Great High Priest, he extends the blessings of royalty and priesthood to commoners like us. Now we are no longer outsiders to the covenant. We were, spiritually speaking, Moabites standing outside the whole system, wondering excruciatingly how we might ever enjoy the blessings of atonement. But now we have been granted insider status. The veil in the temple is torn in two, ushering us into the very presence of God. In fact, the holy of holies is placed by the Spirit into our very selves. Everything about us has changed because of Christmas.

That simple, strawy nativity scene is a reminder that the word is pleading our case forever.

Yes, the priesthood of the believer is a glorious gift of the gospel.

Christ came lowly with us that he might raise us up high with him.

21. His Power and Glory Evermore Proclaim

Today's Gift: Commissioning

"All this is from God, who through Christ reconciled us to himself and gave us the ministry of reconciliation."—2 Corinthians 5:18

If your family is like my family, each member has responsibilities around the Christmas season. As my wife is the raging extrovert with abundant gifts of hospitality and service, she is mainly in charge of all of our holiday get-togethers. Our schedule gets filled with fellowships and dinner parties.

The last few years, she has catered and hosted the staff and pastors' Christmas dinners for our church. She's also in charge of decorating, and she turns even this process into a party, inviting over a few women from the church to help her set up the tree and all the other seasonal accoutrements around the house. (Last year she added a snowy scene with penguins sledding down the staircase railing.)

My job consists largely of lifting heavy things, putting boxes away, setting up any outside décor, determining our Christmas movie-watching schedule, and contributing ideas to the menu planning. It's a pretty cushy gig, and I don't mind it at all. When I was pastoring, a lot of my time in December consisted of preparing Advent sermons and planning our rather elaborate Christmas Eve service. I miss it, and yet I don't.

In your home, maybe someone's in charge of food, another of decorating, another of games, and so on and so forth. We all take on certain responsibilities to help make the celebration of the Christmas season complete and happy for everybody else.

Well, we have responsibilities from Jesus too in connection with the commemoration of his birth. You could say we have jobs to do, but really these directives should be seen as great privileges. It has been this way from the very beginning.

The angels gave the shepherds the privilege of seeing the Christ child and proclaiming his glory. The wise men felt directed by the star to seek out the young Messiah and worship him where they found him. And as Jesus began his ministry, he called disciples into his work and, at the end of it, commissioned them to go into all the world to tell the story of the gospel and help others live in obedience to him too (Matthew 28:19-20).

The entire church is given this glorious privilege as well. We have a job to do, and it is to persist in sharing the good news of the coming of Jesus far and wide.

Now, it's important to remember that the jobs Jesus gives us are not a means by which we earn credit with him. He is not giving us steps *to* salvation. He is giving us the steps *of* salvation—directing us to speak and live according to the work he has already accomplished for us. The good works we are commissioned to do are not how we earn salvation but how we demonstrate that he has earned it for us.

Paul writes in 2 Corinthians 5:18, "All this is from God, who through Christ reconciled us to himself and gave us the ministry of reconciliation." In other words, Jesus has done the great work of reconciliation in uniting us to himself. We receive this reconciliation through faith, but it is a unilateral gift of God's grace. We are not meant to hoard this grace. As Christ has reconciled us to himself, we are now commissioned to work in the ministry of reconciliation. This means seeking to be at peace with all people, loving others as we love ourselves, and announcing the reconciliation with God available to repentant sinners through the power of the gospel.

This is a job to do, sure. But it's also a gift because our generous Jesus has invited us into his work in drawing all people to himself. The power of salvation isn't contingent upon us, but it does work through us as we share the good news with others.

Maybe this Christmas you might think about taking this commissioning more seriously. Maybe we might take the *sharing* of the gospel of Christmas as seriously as we take our enjoyment of the gospel of Christmas for ourselves.

22. Glad and Golden Hours Come Swiftly on the Wing

Today's Gift: Assurance

"I write these things to you who believe in the name of the Son of God, that you may know that you have eternal life."—1 John 5:13

When I was a kid, many of the church people around me excelled in trafficking in fear. For instance, I learned that nearly everything could kill me. Drugs and alcohol and making out with my girlfriend, for instance. But also things like parties or just having the wrong kinds of friends. And I learned that anything could give me a demon. Rock music, certain Saturday-morning cartoons, or even certain toys in the toy box. I lived in a climate of fear and anxiety.

Some of this hand-wringing sounds silly, I know, but it had a devastating impact on my spiritual life because I really didn't need any help in being afraid. I didn't need any help in thinking my salvation was always up in the air. And then Christmas would come around each year, and I was supposed to feel peace and joy, but I just went through it all with a low-grade depression because I was never sure if I was "doing it right." The sentimentality of the season felt strangely at odds with the spiritual discord inside of me.

I carried around with me a sense of not being good enough: of being rejected, disapproved of, not fitting in, not belonging.

It took me a long time to settle more into the *goodness* of the good news. The message of the gospel is that sinners are saved on the basis of what Jesus Christ has done (on the cross and out of the tomb), but for me, it seemed that my security and my assurance of salvation were vitally connected to what I had done. And when you realize that you're constantly aware of your sins and failings, tying your assurance to your accomplishments is a great way to always feel insecure.

I frequently only felt as good as what I hadn't done. I would lie awake at night and stare at the ceiling and wonder, "Am I really his?"

It was later in my Christian life that I discovered that assurance of salvation is also one of the many gifts we get alongside the gift of salvation itself.

I have also learned through my ministry that this lack of assurance is sadly very common. If this sense of spiritual insecurity describes you, I want to say to you, first of all, that *you're normal.*

Can you know that you belong to God? Yes. The apostle John tells us that we can "know" we have eternal life (1 John 5:13). In 2 Corinthians 13:5, Paul says "Examine yourselves to see whether you are in the faith." So if you need some help in answering the definitive question of assurance—"Am I his?"—I think the Bible helps us formulate some diagnostic questions to examine ourselves. So how would you know that you belong to God? If you were going to test yourself, what questions would be on that test?

Here's the first question to ask yourself.

1. Do you find your satisfaction in the eternal more than the earthly?

Now, I don't mean "Do you ever enjoy earthly pleasures?" God has made this world, and he has made it good, and although it is broken and in need of restoration, there are still good gifts from God to be enjoyed here. But these good gifts are not to be enjoyed purely for their own sake but for the glory of the one who made them.

So the deeper question is: where is your hope?

It's ok to have fun with things designed to be fun— to enjoy tasting good food and reading good books and watching good movies and playing in God's creation in a variety of ways—but do these things satisfy you the way only God should? Do you find your satisfaction in the eternal more than the earthly?

Do you think about your spiritual life? Does it impact your thinking and feeling more than the world? Does the reality of God impact how you process your life?

Look, we all mess up in this. It's not about being perfect or perfectly spiritual. It's simply about your ultimate hope. Where do you find your "salvation"? In earthly things or eternal things?

Here's another good question...

2. Do you hate your sin more than its consequences?

Just as it's normal to be afraid of dying, it's normal to hate the consequences of sin—getting caught, getting punished, getting shamed, losing privileges, losing relationships, etc. But everybody hates the consequences of sin. You don't have to have a new nature to hate the consequences of sin. But you *do* have to have a new nature to hate sin itself.

Let me ask you: because it's not enough to simply want to be free of guilt, do you want to be free of sin?

How do you know? If you don't get caught, are you still hurt? Do you experience spiritual conviction?

When you are born again, you are given a new nature. You're given a new heart. You are forgiven, yes, but also the Holy Spirit takes up residence in you and begins to direct your desires. You are being renewed daily.

Your sinful nature is still there too. But you have a new nature that is conforming you more and more to the image of Christ. But if that's true, it doesn't mean that you never sin—you don't become a perfect person; Christians won't be perfected until they join Christ face to face in heaven—but it does mean that your natures are at war, and your new nature is bothered by the old one.

Do you want to, as Paul says in Colossians 3:5, "put to death" what is a part of your earthly nature? Or do you just... not... care?

If you do care, it's a good sign that you have a new nature—that you belong to God, who hates sin and is coming in wrath against it. If you are convicted about your failure to honor God, it's a good sign that you belong to him.

Finally...

3. Do you want Jesus more than heaven?

To live with heaven in view is the highest aspiration you could possibly have. To forsake any temporary satisfaction of this world for the surpassing satisfaction that is found in the glorious world to come is the hardest and yet most pleasurable decision you could ever make.

And yet, to long for a heaven where Jesus is simply incidental is not to long for heaven at all.

Everyone longs for heaven—or a *kind* of heaven. And sometimes the way in which even Christians talk of heaven leaves the impression that it exists more for our glory than for Christ's.

Do you long to see Jesus?

Think of everything you want out of heaven. If Jesus isn't there, is it still heaven?

Let's "right-now-ize" it: Do you want Christmas more than Christ? Are you content experiencing the happiness of a holiday without paying much attention to the happiness of the holy one of Israel?

What do you see when you look to the end? Just you being happy? Or you finally enjoying the embrace of the Savior you claim to walk with now?

And here is how you get to this point—longing more for Jesus than simply for heaven: see what he has accomplished on earth as having been accomplished for you. Look with love at the one who has looked with love at you.

Do you want him? Then you can know that he wants you.

We can know that we have eternal life when we keep looking to Jesus.

23. Born to Give Them Second Birth

Today's Gift: Eternal life

"For the wages of sin is death, but the free gift of God is eternal life in Christ Jesus our Lord."
—*Romans 6:23*

Every Christmas present pales in comparison to the free gift God gives. The gift that he gives us goes right to the heart of human existence.

What does it mean to be fully alive? To be really and truly alive?

Is it enjoying good music? Good food? Health? Money? Is it having a loving family or close friendships? Is it being smart or successful? Being good looking?

All of those answers strike us as good things—and they are good things—but even if these things are what come to mind when we think about what real life is all about, we know deep down they don't quite answer the question, "What does it mean to be fully alive?"

And this is because there are—deep down in the recesses of our hearts and souls, in the darkest corners of our minds—concerns, burdens, and fears that nothing external seems to solve. These are what the philosophers and the psychologists call "existential questions", these questions have less to do with feelings and more to do with our very existence. And, deep down, we somehow understand that these existential questions cannot be answered by superficial living.

Romans 6:23 cuts to the heart of human existence: "For the wages of sin is death, but the free gift of God is eternal life in Christ Jesus our Lord."

Do you know what it means to have eternal life?

It means, of course—as it sounds—to live eternally. To live forever. In John's Gospel we see the moment right before Jesus raises his friend Lazarus from the dead, when he says to Lazarus's sister, "Everyone who lives and believes in me shall never die" (John 11:26). This is, from the lips of Jesus, a reaffirmation of what he has previously said in the most famous Bible verse of all time: "For God so loved the world, that he gave his only Son, that whoever believes in him should not perish but have eternal life" (John 3:16).

To be saved by Jesus is to be saved from the permanence of death; it is to live eternally.

But eternal life means even more than that. It means that when we believe in Jesus, we receive his life put into ours. It means we receive a life that has the quality of eternity—the quality of heaven. To believe in Jesus means having the "Jesus kind of life." It's the kind of change that changes *everything*. It doesn't just answer the question of where we go when we die, but it also answers the questions of our very existence!

The wages of sin is death, but the free gift of God is eternal life through Christ Jesus our Lord! God *really does* forgive sins, and the cross of Christ, where his blood was shed brutally, but freely and *graciously*, is proof that God really does love sinners.

There's nothing you have done or are doing that the blood of Jesus cannot forgive. You are not more powerful a sinner than Jesus is a Savior. If you are covered by the blood of Christ, your sin doesn't lead to death—it is forgiven, canceled, cast into the depths of the sea. Eternal life means forgiveness. Not because you're great but because *he* is. Not because you're a great obeyer but because he's a great forgiver. Not because you're powerful but because the blood of Jesus testifies to our powerful God.

Hebrews 12:24 says that the blood of Jesus "speaks a better word"!

Where the world's messages enslave, the blood cries out, "Freedom."

Where the devil whispers hatred, the blood shouts love.

Where religion says, "Get to work," the blood says, "It is finished."

Where the law says, "Condemned," the blood says, "Forgiven!"

Do you want to be rid of your guilt, free from your sin, and forgiven once for all and for all time? All this is achieved by the blood of Jesus!

Eternal life means freedom, and eternal life means forgiveness, and eternal life means *acceptance*.

When Christ was baptized, the Spirit came down, and the voice bellowed from heaven, "This is my beloved Son, with whom I am well pleased" (Matthew 3:17).

And if you think eternal life couldn't get bigger or better, consider this: what God said at that baptism about his Son Jesus, he says about all his sons and daughters. God's approval of Christ becomes his acceptance of Christians.

In John's Gospel, in chapter 17, Jesus is praying his guts out before his crucifixion, and among many of the staggering things he says in this important prayer, we find these two especially staggering statements: first, Jesus says to the Father, "You ... loved them even as you loved me" (v 23).

And then he says to the Father, "The love with which you have loved me may be in them" (v 26).

Can you wrap your mind around that? That God would love sinners like us in the same way he loves the sinless Jesus?

Have you ever longed for acceptance? Maybe you feel left out, rejected. Maybe you feel that you don't belong. I've felt that way. I still feel that way—more often than I like to admit. I especially felt that way growing up. I never quite fit in with any one group, and even when I did kind of find groups I could hang out with, I still always felt like an outsider. I have felt like an alien everywhere I've ever lived. I've never felt good enough for anybody. If anyone shows me the slightest favor or even love, I'm very suspicious of it.

Ever since I was a little kid, I've longed to feel approved of. For someone to love me *for me*, not for what I can do, or how I can perform, or how smart I can be or how talented, or how I might benefit them, or how I might look.

I think, deep down, that's what all of us really want—for someone to actually truly *know* us and at the same time accept us. Embrace us. Love us.

The one who comes to Jesus, he will not turn away

There is nothing better. Knowing Jesus is what it means to be fully alive. He has made the way to eternal life by his crucifixion and resurrection. He will not reject anyone who comes to him. He has given us eternal life as a free gift.

24. Repeat the Sounding Joy

Today's Gift: Joy

"These things I have spoken to you, that my joy
may be in you, and that your joy may be full."
—*John 15:11*

I'll be honest when I'm telling you that I actually look forward more to Christmas Eve than to Christmas Day. I'm not sure exactly why, but I think it has something to do with the enjoyment of the anticipation. On Christmas Eve, I am still thinking about watching my loved ones opening their gifts or worshiping with my brothers and sisters at the evening candlelight service. This day is a kind of blessed "in between." It's Christmas already but not yet.

Then Christmas Day comes, and it seems to go by in a flash. The floor is littered with the detritus of torn packages and paper. The sink is full of dirty dishes. I start thinking about when I have to go back to work. Christmas Day just can't hold up its end of the holiday.

But Christmas Eve—the holiday magic is still in the air. It's thicker than it will ever get with it.

I wish there was a way for the whole month to feel like Christmas Eve—all of the exuberant joy of the promise without any of the letdown of the reality. I suspect there is. But if I'm going to get to it, I expect I'll have to be thinking about Christmas more deeply than what's happening on the surface.

The most famous holiday story of all time is probably Charles Dickens's *A Christmas Carol*. It's been adapted into a hundred different forms, recycled and reimagined countless times since its publication in 1843. I won't rehearse the entire plot, as you've more than likely seen at least one of those adaptations. But do you remember near the end, when Ebenezer Scrooge finally has his change of heart? He spends the bulk of his adult life—and the reflective journey that takes place in the story—as a miserable miser, greedy and selfish. But at the climactic moment of the story, he awakens to the "true meaning of Christmas" and is saved from his love for money and his hatred for people.

Where does that change ultimately take place? In most versions of the story, the climactic moment occurs in the fourth act when the Ghost of Christmas Future gives Scrooge a glimpse of his future grave. The tombstone is gloomy and neglected. Nobody cares about Scrooge. He has wasted his life not endearing anyone to him. The only people who acknowledge him in his passing are a poor couple whom Dickens depicts as rejoicing at Scrooge's death because he had exploited them in their poverty. The idea is that Scrooge is overcome by the thought of leaving a legacy of greed and never truly having been loved.

I'm sure that that is the straw that broke the camel's back, but I actually think Scrooge's heart change begins in the third act of the story, when the Ghost of Christmas Present shows him the Christmas Eve dinner scene at the home of his impoverished employee Bob Cratchit. It is there that Scrooge sees a family that holds none of the pleasures or luxuries he has equated with the meaning of life, and he is astounded to see them so... happy. In fact, the most impressive sight to Scrooge is that of Cratchit's youngest son, affectionately nicknamed Tiny Tim. This disabled child will not live much longer, the Ghost tells Scrooge, but the miser can see that this boy is unabashedly happy. He is inexplicably, inscrutably happy. He even prays the famous blessing, "God bless us, every one!"

And one reason I know this is the beginning of the end of Ebenezer Scrooge's unregeneracy is that Dickens repeats Tiny Tim's prayer at the very end of the story, after Scrooge has had his Christmas Day awakening. It's not the fear of his own loneliness or poor reputation that really scares Scrooge straight—it's a shocking encounter with unconquerable joy.

What Tiny Tim and the Cratchit family exhibit in their dinner scene is the kind of thing that must come from the deepest well inside of a person. To have nothing and to be threatened with one's very life and *yet to rejoice*... well, that cannot come through natural means. It must come supernaturally.

Jesus tells his followers, "These things I have spoken to you, that my joy may be in you, and that your joy may be full" (John 15:11). What has been Jesus' purpose all along? Why did he come to earth to preach, teach, heal and serve? Why did he come to die and rise again?

To make us more religious? To make us smarter? To make us more moral?

From his own mouth, he says he has done these things that the joy of his very being might be planted inside of us, that our own joy would be overflowing.

This is why the angel declares to those shepherds upon the birth of Jesus, "I bring you good news of great joy" (Luke 2:10).

The good news of the original Christmas Eve is that the real Christmas Day—far from being a letdown—was the greatest day that had ever happened up to that moment. The Christmas Eve gospel is that while all the stuff and the experiences and the feelings might go away moment by moment, the incarnate Christ is real, he is alive, and he is doing work inside of our hearts that will make us thrive when we're weary, hope when we're grieving, and even rejoice when we're suffering.

Jesus isn't blowing smoke. He's not the fog-and-lasers show at your local church production. He is the Lord of the universe, a sure and steady fortress, an eternal help in times of trouble, and the grounds of indomitable and eternal joy—and all with no shadow of turning.

With this joy, you can face whatever Christmas Day is bringing (or not bringing). He is good forever and always. He is more than worth our discovery of enduring happiness in him alone.

25. Glorious Now
Behold Him

Today's Gift: Jesus

"For from his fullness we have all received, grace upon grace."—John 1:16

Sundar Singh was born to a wealthy Indian family in 1889 and enjoyed a relatively carefree childhood with loving parents and a comfortable home. Despite coming from a prominent Sikh family and receiving regular training from a Sadhu (a Sikh ascetic holy man), Singh was sent by his mother to the Christian mission school so that he could learn English.

When he was 14 years old, Singh's mother died, and the grief and pain thrust him into a terrible despair and a terrible rage. He lashed out at the Christian missionaries, ridiculing them and persecuting their converts. So focused was his hatred for the Christian faith, one story has it that in the presence of his friends, he burnt a Bible one page at a time.

The satisfaction of this did not fulfill him, however. That same night he went to lay himself down on the railroad tracks, hoping to end his pain forever. The train never came. But Jesus did.

By dawn, Sundar Singh was a changed man. He confidently told his father that he'd seen a vision of Jesus Christ and that now he aimed to follow the Christian God all of his days. His father begged him to renounce his conversion, but Singh was unmoved. Eventually, his family disowned him, and he was left essentially homeless.

He got baptized on his sixteenth birthday and went to live in a Christian mission for lepers, serving and ministering to the sick. Eventually, Singh made a full commitment to a life of homelessness, renouncing all possessions, in the hopes of truly walking and living as Jesus walked and lived. He wanted to bring the gospel to his fellow Indians, in the guise of their own culture, so he modeled himself after a Sadhu, becoming a Jesus-worshiping, Jesus-following, Jesus-preaching Indian ascetic mystic.

Here was a guy who, like Paul, had hated Jesus and hated Jesus' church, yet found his life invaded by Jesus when he least expected it. And Sundar Singh renounced everything that prevented him from becoming more like Jesus. One fateful day, Singh began an annual trek up the mountains to Tibet, never to be seen again. He simply disappeared.

Here's a rather poignant anecdote from Sundar Singh's life:

> *"He was asked once by a Hindu professor what it was that he had found in Christianity that he had not found in his old religion. 'I have found Christ,' Sundar Singh said.*

*"'Oh yes, I know,' said the confused professor.
'But what particular doctrine or principle have
you found that you did not have before?'*

*"'The particular thing I have found,' Sundar
Singh replied, 'is Christ.'"*

Christmas Day has come, and it is going to go by quickly. It will be behind us soon enough, and perhaps so will our hopes for feeling something... *different* this year.

Every year in the days leading up to this day, I walk through the local stores doing my Christmas shopping, and I am struck by all of the implicit acknowledgments of the beauty of the gospel. Everything from wrapping paper to greeting cards, from sweatshirts to gigantic cardboard signs hanging from the ceiling announces one-word aspirational virtues: Joy. Peace. Love. Hope.

For the unbeliever, the promise of Christmas is the promise of "spiritual vibes."

Everybody wants peace on earth. Very few see the appeal of the narrow way of the Prince of Peace.

Because the truth is that we cannot have any of these beautiful virtues apart from their perfect embodiment in Jesus Christ. Christmas is not about warm fuzzies; it is about the one who finally delivers on the promise of everything we acknowledge as good and true.

The Bible will not let us have ethereal virtues.

Do you want peace? Christ himself is our peace (Ephesians 2:14).

Do you want love? Christ himself is love (1 John 4:8).

Do you want hope? Christ himself is our hope (Titus 2:13).

In John 1:16, the apostle tells us that "from his fullness we have all received, grace upon grace."

He is an endless fountain of the blessings of grace. Jesus is the apex and sum of all that is good and beautiful. He is the culmination of all that we really need, and more. Indeed, if we were to have every gift we've explored since December 1 except the gift of Jesus himself, we would still be as poor as ever. Because everything *without Christ* is a heap of nothing.

We have nothing apart from Jesus.

When the feeble scaffolding of our religious efforts and emotional spirituality falls away, may we be found claiming only Christ. Only Christ.

He alone has died for our sins. He alone has risen to conquer death and purchase for us eternal life. He alone has ascended to the Father to sit at his right hand and constantly intercede for us. He alone is returning in great glory (very soon) to finally consummate his kingdom and vanquish sin, grief, and death forever. He alone will reign as the lamp of the new creation. He alone is worthy, worthy, worthy.

And so today and every day we can come to the endless fountain of grace in Christ. We can look upon his face, because he is always warm and kind, gentle and loving (2 Corinthians 4:6). We can take his hand, because he is always steady and strong, sure and invincible (Psalm 73:23). We can follow him, even unto death, because he always lives.

We can come to him not simply for forgiveness, but also for righteousness (1 Corinthians 1:30). He has dressed us in the wedding garment of his own work, for ours are filthy rags.

On this Christmas Day, turn out your pockets, brothers and sisters, and offer him nothing but your need, and he will give you the riches of the righteousness of himself. He will give you *himself.*

As Augustine once said, *You ask for your reward and the Giver is himself the gift. What more could you want?*

Notes on
Chapter Titles

Each of the devotion titles is taken from the lyrics of a Christmas carol. The songs sourced are as follows:

1. O Holy Night
2. O Little Town of Bethlehem
3. What Child Is This?
4. O Little Town of Bethlehem
5. Come, Thou Long-Expected Jesus
6. While Shepherds Watched Their Flocks
7. Hark! The Herald Angels Sing
8. O Come, All Ye Faithful
9. The First Noel
10. Joy to the World
11. O Little Town of Bethlehem
12. Angels from the Realms of Glory
13. O Holy Night
14. Hark! The Herald Angels Sing
15. It Came upon the Midnight Clear
16. Hark! The Herald Angels Sing
17. Away in a Manger
18. O Holy Night
19. O Come, O Come, Emmanuel
20. What Child Is This?

21. O Holy Night
22. It Came upon the Midnight Clear
23. Hark! The Herald Angels Sing
24. Joy to the World
25. We Three Kings

thegoodbook
COMPANY

BIBLICAL | RELEVANT | ACCESSIBLE

At The Good Book Company, we are dedicated to helping Christians and local churches grow. We believe that God's growth process always starts with hearing clearly what he has said to us through his timeless word—the Bible.

Ever since we opened our doors in 1991, we have been striving to produce Bible-based resources that bring glory to God. We have grown to become an international provider of user-friendly resources to the Christian community, with believers of all backgrounds and denominations using our books, Bible studies, devotionals, evangelistic resources, and DVD-based courses.

We want to equip ordinary Christians to live for Christ day by day, and churches to grow in their knowledge of God, their love for one another, and the effectiveness of their outreach.

Call us for a discussion of your needs or visit one of our local websites for more information on the resources and services we provide.

Your friends at The Good Book Company

thegoodbook.com | thegoodbook.co.uk
thegoodbook.com.au | thegoodbook.co.nz
thegoodbook.co.in